Canadian Biography Series

ALICE MUNRO: A DOUBLE LIFE

Alice Munro, in 1990.
This picture, taken by Jerry Bauer, was
used for the cover of Friend of My Youth.

Alice Munro
A DOUBLE LIFE

Catherine Sheldrick Ross

ECW PRESS

Copyright © ECW PRESS, 1992

CANADIAN CATALOGUING IN PUBLICATION DATA

Ross, Catherine Sheldrick
Alice Munro : a double life

(Canadian biography series ; no. 1)
Includes bibliographical references.
ISBN 1-55022-153-1

1. Munro, Alice, 1931–   – Biography. 2. Authors,
Canadian (English) – 20th century – Biography.*
I. Title. II. Series: Canadian biography series
(Toronto, Ont.) ; no. 1

PS8576.U5Z84 1992   C813'.54   C92-093375-0
PR9199.3.M8Z84 1992

This book has been published with the assistance of grants
from the The Canada Council and the Ontario Arts Council.

Design and imaging by ECW Type & Art, Oakville, Ontario.
Printed by Hignell Printing Limited, Winnipeg, Manitoba.

Distributed by General Publishing Co. Limited
30 Lesmill Road, Toronto, Ontario M3B 2T6

Published by ECW PRESS,
1980 Queen Street East, 2nd Floor, Toronto, Ontario M4L 1J2

ACKNOWLEDGEMENTS

A number of people helped with this book. Thanks are due to Thomas Tausky and Laurie Kruk for giving me access to their interview material; to Special Collections, University of Calgary Libraries, for photographs and for access to archival material; to James Munro for providing photographs and for permission to reproduce a Munro's Books bookmark; to McClelland and Stewart for photographs; and, of course, to Alice Munro and Gerry Fremlin.

The frontispiece and illustration 14, photographs by Jerry Bauer, are provided courtesy of the Canadian Publishers, McClelland and Stewart; illustration 2 is provided by the Regional Collection, University of Western Ontario; photographs 3, 4, 5, and 7 are provided courtesy of Alice Munro; photographs 6, 9, 10, and 11 are provided courtesy of James Munro; illustrations 8, 12, and 13 are reproduced by permission of Special Collections, University of Calgary Libraries.

TABLE OF CONTENTS

ACKNOWLEDGEMENTS 5

LIST OF ILLUSTRATIONS 8

CHRONOLOGY 9

Alice Munro: A Double Life 15

WORKS CONSULTED 94

LIST OF ILLUSTRATIONS

1. Alice Munro, in 1990 . . . . *frontispiece*
2. A Fire Insurance Plan for Wingham 22
3. Alice as a baby 25
4. Alice about three years old 32
5. Wedding picture 50
6. Jim and Alice on Grouse Mountain 51
7. Alice in West Vancouver 54
8. The opening page of "Death of a White Fox" 59
9. The Munro family, circa 1963 62
10. Alice working in the bookstore 63
11. Bookmark for Munro's Books 66
12. Holograph sketch of Jubilee 70
13. A draft of the last page of *Lives of Girls and Women* . . . 72
14. Alice Munro, in 1990 90

Chronology

1830–50   The bush area of the Huron Tract, located in south-western Ontario, is opened to settlement. In the 1850s, three brothers named Laidlaw leave Halton County to settle in Morris Township, in Huron County. A falling tree kills one brother as he is clearing the land for farming; another brother is Alice Laidlaw's grandfather.

1898   Anne Clarke Chamney is born. She grows up on a poor farm near Carleton Place in the Ottawa Valley.

1901   Robert Eric Laidlaw is born and grows up on a farm near Blyth, Ontario, in Huron County.

1925   Robert Laidlaw buys his first pair of silver foxes and begins to breed them on his father's farm.

1927   Anne Clarke Chamney marries Robert Laidlaw, her third cousin, and they settle on a nine-acre farm in Turnberry Township on the Maitland River, just west of Wingham.

1929   The stock market crashes, beginning a 10-year economic depression.

1931   Alice Ann is born, on Friday, 10 July, to Anne and Robert Laidlaw.

1936   Bill, Alice's brother, is born.

1937   Alice starts school at the Lower Town School, which she attends for two years. Sheila, Alice's sister, is born.

1939   Alice starts grade four at the Wingham Public School. World War II begins, and Canada enters the war against Germany.

1941   Alice travels with her father to the Pine Tree Hotel in Muskoka, north of Orillia, where her mother has been selling fox furs to the American summer tourists.

1943	It is recognized that Alice's mother is very ill, although Parkinson's disease is not diagnosed till some years later.
1944	Alice enters grade nine in the Wingham and District High School. Alice's paternal grandmother and great-aunt move to Wingham to help out the Laidlaw family.
1945	In May, Germany signs terms of unconditional surrender. Wingham's 99th Battery comes home in December.
1947	On 5 April, the Maitland River has its worst flood since 1912, and families in Lower Wingham have to be evacuated from their homes on Easter Day. Robert Laidlaw winds down the failing fox-farm operation, and starts a job as a night watchman at the foundry, where he works for two years.
1948	In the summer, Alice works as a maid for a family in Rosedale, a wealthy part of Toronto. Alice receives the Dominion-Provincial Bursary for grade 13 students at the December commencement exercise at Wingham High School. Alice Laidlaw and Mary Ross tie for the Marion I. Whyte Memorial Scholarship for Middle School French.
1949	Alice enters the journalism program at the University of Western Ontario, having won a two-year tuition scholarship and a bursary. While at university, she works part-time at the London Public Library and at Western's Lawson Library.
1950	In the summer between Alice's first and second years at Western, she works as a waitress in a lodge in Muskoka. In her second year, she switches to a major in English. Her first short story is published: "The Dimensions of a Shadow" appears in *Folio*, Western's literary magazine.
1951	Alice marries James (Jim) Armstrong Munro in Wingham on Saturday, 29 December. They move to Vancouver, where Jim works for Eaton's Department Store for the next 12 years.

1952	Alice starts work in February as a part-time assistant in the Vancouver Public Library. In September she begins to work full-time. Robert Laidlaw starts poultry farming, later choosing to farm turkeys exclusively.
1953	A daughter, Sheila Margaret, is born to Alice and Jim Munro on 5 October. A first magazine sale, the story "A Basket of Strawberries," is made to *Mayfair*.
1954	A story entitled "The Strangers," written in the spring of 1951, is sold to Robert Weaver for the CBC radio programme *Trans-Canada Matinee*. During the 1950s and 1960s, Alice publishes stories at the rate of one or two a year in Canadian periodicals including *Chatelaine*, *Tamarack Review*, *Montrealer*, *Canadian Forum*, and *Queen's Quarterly*.
1955	A daughter, Catherine, is born, but dies within two days.
1957	A daughter, Jenny Allison, is born on 4 June.
1959	Anne Clarke Chamney Laidlaw dies after a long struggle with Parkinson's disease. Alice writes sections of a novel, variously titled "Death of a White Fox" and "The Norwegian," that is never completed.
1963	Jim and Alice move with their family to Victoria and establish a bookstore, Munro's Books.
1966	The Munro family moves to a new house on Rockland Avenue. A daughter, Andrea Sarah, is born on 8 September.
1968	*Dance of the Happy Shades* is published, and subsequently wins a Governor-General's Award.
1971	*Lives of Girls and Women* is published, and in 1972 it wins the Canadian Booksellers' Award. Book-of-the-Month Club chooses *Lives* as an alternate selection in 1973.
1973	The marriage dissolves, and Jim and Alice separate. Alice teaches creative writing at Notre Dame University in Nelson, British Columbia, for the summer. In September, she moves to London, Ontario, with

Jenny and Andrea. For a time, she commutes from London to Toronto to teach creative writing at York University.

1974   Alice is writer in residence for the academic year 1974–75 at the University of Western Ontario. Gerry Fremlin and Alice Munro meet again, for the first time since they were students together at Western. *Something I've Been Meaning to Tell You* is published.

1975   Alice moves to Clinton, Ontario, 20 miles south of Wingham, to live with Gerry Fremlin.

1976   Robert Laidlaw dies in a Toronto hospital after a heart operation. Alice receives the honorary degree of Doctor of Letters at spring convocation at the University of Western Ontario. Virginia Barber of New York becomes Alice's literary agent, and sells her stories to the *New Yorker*; it is the beginning of a long-standing connection. The divorce between Jim and Alice Munro is formalized in 1976. Alice marries Gerald Fremlin. Jim also remarries.

1977   Alice's screenplay *1847: The Irish* is shot in the summer, and is broadcast in 1978 as part of the CBC television series *The Newcomers; Les Arrivants*.

1978   *Who Do You Think You Are?* is published, and wins a Governor General's Award. Published as *The Beggar Maid: Stories of Flo and Rose* in the United States and the United Kingdom, this collection is shortlisted for the Booker Prize.

1979   Alice tours Australia in March 1979. The trip is part of the Canada-Australia Literary Prize, which Alice wins in 1977, and which is awarded jointly by the Australia Council and Canadian External Affairs. Robert Laidlaw's novel, *The McGregors: A Novel of an Ontario Pioneer Family*, is published posthumously by Alice's publisher, Macmillan.

1980   Alice is writer in residence at the University of British Columbia between January and April. From September to October, she is writer in residence at the University of Queensland in Australia.

1981	Alice travels to the Republic of China with some other Canadian writers, and celebrates her fiftieth birthday there in July.
1982	*The Moons of Jupiter* is published. Alice tours Norway, Denmark, and Sweden to promote the release of the Norwegian translation of *Who Do You Think You Are?* entitled *Tiggerkiken* ("Beggarmaid"). A conference on Alice Munro is held at the University of Waterloo, the proceedings of which are published as *The Art of Alice Munro: Saying the Unsayable*, edited by Judith Miller.
1984	The Atlantis Films adaptation of Alice's "Boys and Girls" wins an Oscar in the live-action-short category.
1986	*The Progress of Love* is published, and wins a Governor General's Award. Alice is the first winner of the Marian Engel Award, given to a woman writer for an outstanding body of work.
1990	*Friend of My Youth* is published. To raise funds for the Blyth Festival, "Alice Munro and friends" write "Lights Out at Camp Ketchakellor," to be presented at a dinner theatre 21–22 September 1990.
1991	*Friend of My Youth* makes the shortlist for the Governor General's Award, and wins the Trillium Book Award of $10,000 for the best book published in 1990 by an Ontario author. It also wins the Commonwealth Writers' Prize (Canada and Caribbean region). In April, Alice is awarded the 1990 Canada Council Molson prize of $50,000 for her "outstanding lifetime contribution to the cultural and intellectual life of Canada." Alice's daughter Sheila has a son — Alice's first grandchild.

Alice Munro

A DOUBLE LIFE

ALICE LAIDLAW ALWAYS KNEW what she wanted to be — very, very famous. As a young child, she had gorgeous daydreams about herself as a glittering movie star in a "blue velvet dress" (unpublished interview [Tausky]). When she was nine, she decided to become a famous writer instead. Not an unusual ambition, though certainly not encouraged in the reticent, self-effacing Scots-Irish community of Wingham, Ontario, where Alice grew up in the 1930s and '40s. The only unusual thing is that she succeeded magnificently.

And what is she famous for? For stories written with such emotional honesty, compassion, and intimacy that in them readers recognize their deepest selves. For stories so rich they seem like compressed novels, juxtaposing past against present, one point of view against another. For creating an identifiable "Munro country" based on her own experience of Huron County, Ontario. For presenting ordinary life so that it appears luminous, invested with a kind of magic. Perhaps more than anyone else, Munro is responsible for making short-story writing respectable in Canada. A generation of short-story writers in Canada has been encouraged by her example. Writer Joan Clark has said, "she's the best short story writer, bar none, that we have in the country, and if I'm going to be influenced by any writer, I'd just as soon be influenced by the best." Carol Shields agrees: "I'm an enormous fan of Alice Munro's. . . . Her use of language is very sophisticated, but I can always hear, underlying the sentence and its rhythms, that rural Ontario sound." Critics have praised her visionary lyricism and dazzlingly paradoxical style, her sure knowledge of the entanglements of human feeling, and her construction of stories from small moments of illumination and recognition. A recent computer search for articles, interviews, and reviews published on Munro produced a list of citations 41 pages long. The one thing all these sources agreed on is Alice Munro's place as one of the world's major writers of short stories.

When I went to Clinton, Ontario, in June 1991 to interview Munro for this book, she was just home from Toronto, where she had attended a cocktail party held to celebrate her winning the $50,000 Molson Prize. And what, I asked her, does she think now about being famous? "Granted wishes," she said laughing, referring to those children in fairy tales whose comeuppance is to get exactly what they have asked for. With about six requests a day to make public appearances, give readings, judge contests, offer opinions, and grant interviews, she sometimes fantasizes about escaping her public role. Perhaps she could live off by herself, with her family and friends, and write books under some name that nobody would know — perhaps just A.M. In fact, she lives with her second husband in a white frame house, with nasturtiums, blue delphiniums, raspberry canes, a birdbath, and lots of trees in the big backyard. I remarked that her life is deliberately removed from the bizarre life of the artist. Her answer: "It's like that comment by Flaubert: 'Live an orderly way like a bourgeois so that you can be violent and original in your work'" (unpublished interview [Ross]).

In person, she is warm, intense, and amusing. Unlike the women, recently endorsed by Carolyn Heilbrun, who "disdain those efforts of dress, cosmetics, and hairdressing," let themselves go, and successfully separate their personhood from their sexual appeal (Heilbrun 54), Alice has said, "How I look matters a great deal" ("Great Dames" 38). Pictures on book jackets show an attractive woman with a beautiful smile and dark, curly hair, cut longer in the 1970s and stylishly short in the 1990s (fig. 1). She is "articulate, humorous, and approachable," says Jeri Kroll (qtd. in Munro, "Interview" 49); "She never misses a nuance of interaction going on about her," says Adele Wiseman (103); "a complicated woman of many poses," says Beverly Rasporich (2).

"The Twin Choices of My Life"

Where Alice grew up, admitting that you wanted fame would be just asking for trouble. "Who do you think you are?" people would say to take you down a peg. In Huron County, the minute you revealed ambition, Munro recalls, the response was "to [slap] down your confidence at every possible point that it emerge[d]" ("Name" 69). As Del Jordan explains in *Lives of Girls and Women*: "to be ambitious was to court failure and to risk making a fool of oneself. The worst thing, I gathered, the worst thing that could happen in this life was to have people laughing at you" (32). For Scots Presbyterians, wanting to be remarkable would certainly seem to be an imprudent challenge to fate — those "supernatural powers always on the lookout for greed" (71). So Alice learned early to keep her ambition to herself, and to put on a mask of ordinariness: "I always did value myself terribly, but I had to pretend I didn't for purposes of disguise in a world that we all have to cope with" ("Name" 72).

Thus developed what would become a lifelong split between ordinary life and the secret life of the imagination. In a 1984 interview with Thomas Tausky, Munro suggested that this split was the theme of her first, unfinished novel:

> The novel that I had all planned in my teens I still think about. I can see how clearly it relates . . . I can now see some significance in it. It's very dark; it's very imitative and very Gothic. . . . It's about a girl called Charlotte Muir, and [her name] is the title of the book. And Charlotte is living in a lonely place off by herself — very *Wuthering Heights*y. And she doesn't go to school. She's reputed by the villagers and farm people to be a witch, or weird and witchlike. And she hooks in a farm boy and decides to make him fall in love with her. They become engaged, and this is her way of redeeming herself and getting herself into ordinary life. I think she is living alone. He's kind of freckle-faced; he's not a romantic hero. There's lots of Gothic stuff in here!
>
> Along comes a preacher [laughter] who is probably the *Scarlet Letter* man — the dark, powerful, Puritanical, sexually attractive preacher who immediately establishes

himself as the enemy of the heroine in the community and breaks up her engagement. I hadn't read *The Scarlet Letter* by this time but all these strains were getting to me. He breaks up her relationship and takes away her hope of normal life by forbidding this fellow to marry her. Then I think she gets mad and puts a curse on the preacher, because she really has powers. The preacher is dying. She now realizes that she is in love with him or, at least, she wants the curse to be removed from him. . . . *Then*, then, the only way she can remove the curse from the preacher is to take it on herself, which she does. So she saves his life by condemning herself. She then dies. The only parts I think I wrote are deathbed scenes. She dies and then I think the preacher realizes he's in love with her after she's dead. It's *Wuthering Heights*y then — it's united in death. But I can see what was going on. I can see that these were the twin choices of my life, which were marriage and mother-hood or the black life of the artist. I was aware of that and I was working with it fictionally before I had any idea of it. (9–10)

In conventional depictions of women's lives, at least until recently, women have husbands and children *or* they can be artists; they can't have both love and art. Norma Shearer, in *The Red Shoes*, might want to dance and wear entrancing red ballet slippers and also be married to a handsome orchestra conductor, but she has to choose. Alice Laidlaw wanted both. Her subsequent career has been a balancing act of responding to these contradictory claims of art and of marriage and mother-hood. As she remarked to John Metcalf, "there is probably a contradiction in many women writers in the woman *herself*. . . . Between the woman who is ambitious and the woman who . . . is passive, who wants to be dominated, who wants to have someone between her and the world. And I know *I'm* like this. I have the two women" ("Conversation" 59).

"A Very Deceptive Life"

In many interviews conducted over a span of decades, Munro has talked about her strategy of holding onto "the two women" by leading parallel and separate lives. Unlike Charlotte Muir, whose dark powers are known and feared, Alice Laidlaw prudently tried to keep her powers and ambitions to herself. In childhood, what did these powers consist of? A love of language and a sensuous appreciation for words; a watchful, observing, noticing nature; and a vivid memory for the details of how things looked, smelled, sounded, and felt. And her ambition? "From the age of 11, art was my religion. . . . Nothing in my life seemed more important to me" (qtd. in Timson 67). This vocation was secret. As she told Eleanor Wachtel in 1990, "I very early on got the notion that my real life had to be hidden, had to be protected. I didn't think you could go to your teacher or your parents, and tell them what you really thought about anything. . . . I just, I suppose, lived a very deceptive life" ("Interview" 48). Telling her own life story to interviewers, she consistently uses the motifs of the spy story: deception, disguises, the role of the detached watcher, and the contrast between the life of appearance and the real, secret life. In 1973, she told Barbara Frum how she used to placate the outside world in order to avoid ridicule and gain time for work.

And so I began very early to behave in a disguised way. I wanted to be a writer from the time I was 12 yet I never told anybody. The work was always a very private thing that I felt I had to protect. And then when I got married quite young and started having kids and lived in the suburbs, I went on protecting it and living two completely different lives — the real and absolutely solitary life and the life of appearances. I worked out a way of living by pretending to be what people wanted me to be . . . . I wouldn't tell anyone I was writing. ("Great Dames" 32)

Living a secret life was not, in the beginning, so much of a problem. Alice was a buoyant child with a desire to be noticed and a lot of confidence in her own powers: "I think as a child I always felt separate, but pretty happy to be so — and manipulating people and events pretty satisfactorily" (unpublished interview [Tausky]). Later, in high school, Munro recalls that writing still gave her the sense that she could cope with anything: "I really felt so buoyed up, so excited by this writing thing that I had latched on to. It gave me in those years the most enormous happiness. More than it ever did after I began to grasp what it really was all about. I was quite stunned by what I was able to do at 15 or 16" (unpublished interview [Tausky]). However, during high school, which is also a time for the serious business of discovering adult roles, Alice wanted desperately to be the kind of girl who gets asked to dances. She told Tausky about her later years in high school:

I began to feel terribly out of things and superficially very unhappy about that, because I wanted to be an ordinary girl. I wanted to be very attractive to boys and I wanted to go out. I wanted to get married, to get a diamond — those things — more or less as signs of being a fully okay kind of woman. And then . . . the plan to write got crystallized about puberty too. I was actually doing it at age 14 or 15. I was doing it all the time. (unpublished interview)

The high-school girl who wanted to be attractive to boys went on to experience those other proofs of normal womanhood: university, marriage, children, married turbulence, new relationships, and remarriage. Shadowing this life, however, was always the watcher who stands outside it to observe and to turn it into art. The relationship between these two women is complex, because one woman's life is the subject matter of the other's writing. Unlike another of Canada's celebrated short-story writers, Mavis Gallant, who deliberately avoided marriage and children so that she would be able to write, Alice Munro has used her life as daughter, wife, suburban homemaker, and mother as raw material. Like Del in *Lives of Girls and Women*, she subversively takes the unsuspecting world, to "turn it into black fable and tie it up in my novel" (206). She sees herself as a spy, leading a double life, only pretending to be like everyone else. The idea of a hidden identity appears in many early stories in the form of a watchful child observer, where watching is associated with shame, betrayal, and exposure. In later books, the idea of a hidden identity appears as a fascination with the theme of adultery and the "double life it creates, especially for a married wife and mother who is expected to live her life for other people. Instead, she can be living this secret, exploratory life" (qtd. in Timson 67).

Alice Munro Country

The area of Huron County around Wingham is known internationally as Alice Munro country. With its horror of disclosure, this is the last place to want to celebrate itself or have its secrets exposed. Nevertheless, as the setting for many Munro stories, and variously called Jubilee, Hanratty, and Dalgleish, the town of Wingham has passed into art along with some other Ontario towns: Sara Jeannette Duncan's Elgin, Stephen Leacock's Mariposa, James Reaney's Stratford, and Robertson Davies's Deptford. Robert Thacker calls Munro's Huron County "a place remembered, recovered, revised, and, at times, renounced" (214). This small town of about 3,000 people is only approximately 125 miles from Toronto, 70 miles from London, and 25 miles from the lake-port town of Goderich. Despite being at the junction of two highways and having its own CBC radio station, Wingham seems somehow remote. As the narrator put it in Munro's "The Peace of Utrecht," "there is no easy way to get to Jubilee from anywhere on earth" (Dance 196).

This is the town in which Alice was born on 10 July 1931, as announced in the Wingham Advance-Times (16 July 1931): "Born. Laidlaw. In Wingham General Hospital on Friday, July 10th, to Mr. and Mrs. R.E. Laidlaw, a daughter Alice Ann." The weekly Wingham Advance-Times, published each Thursday, has recorded the life of this community for more than a century — conservative, conscious of decorum, yet apparently prone to violent injury and sudden death. In the week of Alice's birth, the paper reports road building ("The connecting link in the

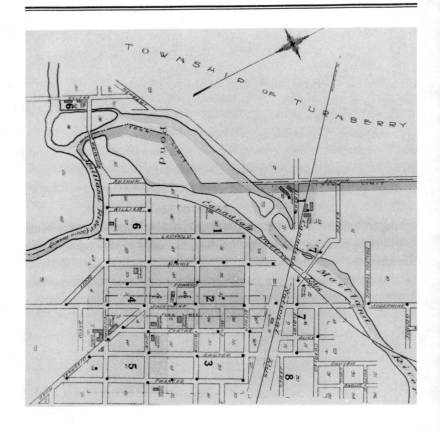

FIGURE 2

A fire-insurance plan for Wingham, Ontario, produced by the Underwriters' Survey Bureau in 1904, revised in 1928.

Provincial pavement from Clinton to London was opened a week ago"), a wedding ("An exceeding pretty July wedding was solemnified"), an accident ("Fall down Cellar Stairway"), obituaries ("It was with deep regret that the community learned of the sudden death . . ."), and agricultural news ("Turkey breeding is not the difficult undertaking that is generally supposed" [9 July 1931]). This is the community in which Alice grew up, the community she knows in her bones and has made her own in her fiction. The map of Wingham, from a fire-insurance plan created in 1904 and revised in 1928 (fig. 2), shows local landmarks described in various Munro stories: the town hall on Josephine Street, with its great bell ready "to be rung in the event of some mythical disaster" (*Dance* 196); the United, Anglican, and Presbyterian churches described in "Age of Faith" (*Lives*); the CNR station from which Rose takes the train to Toronto in "Wild Swans" (*Who Do You Think You Are?*); the skating rink described in "The Moon in the Orange Street Skating Rink" (*The Progress of Love*); Alice's public school, which has an annual March concert like the one depicted in *Lives*; and the foundry, described in "Working for a Living," where Robert Laidlaw worked in the late 1940s.

"Whatever Myths You Want"

The Laidlaw family didn't live in Wingham itself, but a mile or so west, in a "legendary non-part of town called Lower Town (pronounced Loretown)" ("Everything"). Until around 1873, Lower Town was more important than Wingham. Then Wingham got the railway and expanded, while Lower Town went downhill to become a rural slum. As Munro told Alan Twigg (and was forthwith sternly taken to task for the following disclosures by the Wingham paper), "We lived outside the whole social structure. . . . We lived in this kind of little ghetto where all the bootleggers and prostitutes and hangers-on lived. Those were the people I knew. It was a community of outcasts. I had that feeling about myself" ("What Is" 18). The Laidlaws lived in a red-brick Ontario farmhouse on a nine-acre farm. A photograph taken at the side of this house in the fall of 1931 shows a smiling Alice, about three months old, held in her mother's lap (fig. 3). This house is described, as remembered from childhood, in the uncollected story "Home": "All the rooms are small. . . . The wallpaper in the front rooms was palely splotched by a leaky chimney. The floors were of wide boards which my mother painted green or brown or yellow every spring; in the middle was a square of linoleum . . ." (135). When the leaves were off the trees, the view eastward included church spires and the square, brick tower of the Wingham town hall. The area behind the farmhouse is now filled with wrecked cars — the house has been sold, and the current owners have rented it to people with a wrecking business. But when Alice was growing up, the view behind the house was of a wide field and flats that sloped down to the curve of the river.

This river flowed past the foot of the Laidlaw property on its way from Wingham to Lake Huron at Goderich. Indians had called it Meneseteung before it was renamed the Maitland. With its spring floods, the river took on a legendary quality for Alice as she grew up. This little stretch of river, she says, "will provide whatever myths you want, whatever adventures. . . . This ordinary place is sufficient, everything here touchable and mysterious" ("Everything").

> Downstream to the west, and visible from our place, a wide curve of the river had broadened the flats, and to the north, it had undercut a high steep bank covered with trees. . . . To the south . . . the village of Zetland once thrived — remembered my father, but in my time utterly vanished. . . . This scene . . . was my first access to the countryside of southern Ontario, which was and has remained magical. ("Walk" 38)

The farm, the mile or so of river, Wingham, and the nearby towns of Goderich and Blyth provided the geography of Alice's childhood world, later celebrated in her stories. Munro has summed up the culture of her area of Huron County as a

FIGURE 3

"Mrs. Robbie Laidlaw and one of her children."
Alice is a few months old in autumn 1931.

rural culture with strong Scots-Irish background. . . . that has become fairly stagnant. With a big sense of righteousness. But with big bustings-out and grotesque crime. And ferocious sexual humour and the habit of getting drunk and killing each other off on the roads. . . . I always think the country I was born and brought up in is full of event and emotions and amazing things going on all the time. ("Interview" [Hancock] 93)

Some writers might find this landscape raw and unpromising. But when Munro looks at Huron County, she sees a whole geology and archaeology of meaning. Like the teacher Mr. Cleaver in the uncollected story "Characters," she is very aware of "the landscape under the one you see" — "the lakes of former times, the old abandoned shores" (73, 72). She has an archaeological sense of layers of human history. In "Names," a piece now held in the Alice Munro Papers at the University of Calgary, and originally written to accompany Peter d'Angelo's unpublished "Ontario Photo Album," Munro notes:

Somebody tried to write a history of the town and the townships around. It was all names, crowding over one another. Names of buildings, names of people. Industries, businesses, railways. . . . Things pile on top, and who cares? History seems a gentle avocation, orderly and consoling, until you get further into it. Then you see the shambles, the prodigal, dizzying, discouraging confusion. Just here, just on this one patch of the earth's surface where things have not been piling up for very long; so what does that say about the rest? Nevertheless some people will continue; some people are fired with the lasting hope of getting things straight.

Obviously one of these people who wants to get things straight, Munro has spent her writing career recording the lives of Huron county saints, including her own family, going back several generations.

The Laidlaws: "An Extraordinary Timidity"

Alice's own story starts not in Wingham in 1931, but in Scotland and Ireland. It involves the intersection of two families with very different traditions. Her mother's family was ambitious, self-confident, and self-dramatizing, much like the travelling Chaddeley cousins in "Connection" (*The Moons of Jupiter*), who saw life in terms of change and possibility. Her father's family, like the Fleming sisters in "The Stone in the Field" (*Moons*) was diligent, self-controlled, and self-denying, seeing life in terms of ritualized work for its own sake. Her mother's family, the Chamneys, with the latitude of the Irish and of the Church of England, liked to sing, dance, and take a drink (Rasporich 5). Her father's family were Presbyterian Scots, "against the English Church and the Family Compact, Bishop Strachan, and saloons" ("Working" 15).

On the Laidlaw side, Alice Munro's grandfather's grandfather had come from Scotland, from the Vale of Ettrick, described to me by Munro as incredibly beautiful, "an archetypal place to have come from." "They lived right at the head of the valley, of course in the poorest possible place" (unpublished interview [Ross]). Munro has traced the early family history of the Laidlaws with the idea of writing about it some day. She discovered that in Scotland the family were shepherds and farm workers, but they were also great letter writers. After they came to Canada by ship in 1818, they wrote home to Scotland letters filled with vivid descriptions of the voyage, their impressions of Toronto in the 1820s, and their first farm near Milton in Halton County. In Scotland, the family had been unlucky financially, but in Canada it divided, with one branch becoming very rich and Alice's branch staying poor. Her great-great-grandfather went to Joliet near Chicago, aiming to make his fortune as an American. In 1839, almost as soon as he got there, he died of cholera during an epidemic. He left behind him a widow, a baby — born on the day of his death — and five older children. His brothers, who had stayed behind in Halton County, had to go down to the United States by ox cart to bring the bereaved family back to Ontario, where they would thereafter be disadvantaged. In the early 1850s, the three sons of this family left

Halton County and came to Morris Township in Huron County. There they got crown land near Blyth and started farming. The other branch of the family "went on to Toronto and became The Laidlaws, with the lumberyard and the trucks" (in the July 1991 *Report on Business Magazine*'s listing of Canada's top companies, Laidlaw Incorporated ranked seventeenth out of a thousand for profitability in 1990).

It seemed as if Alice's great-great-grandfather was punished for his presumption in daring too much. From that time on, Alice claims, in his branch of the family, there was "timidity, caution, sisters that couldn't speak to anybody. I think of it all as some kind of psychological effect of the trauma." Other hardships took their toll. In Morris Township, a falling tree killed the older brother almost immediately as he tried to clear his land. The other two brothers married, began families, and struggled to establish pioneer farms. Munro says she has letters written by her great-grandfather, Thomas Laidlaw, describing how he had to leave his own farm and work for the summer for someone else to make enough money to survive: "He walked down south to Middlesex County and he was starving. He had to ask someone at a farmhouse to go and give him a bowl of milk. He got work. He saved enough money to come back and spend the winter clearing and homesteading" (unpublished interview [Ross]). In the story "The Stone in the Field," the narrator's father, in hospital for the last time with heart disease, becomes reminiscent and recalls those ancestors who faced death by falling trees and cholera: "I think the courage got burnt out of them. Their religion did them in, and their upbringing. . . . Pride was what they had when they had no more gumption" (*Moons* 30–31).

Alice's own father, Robert Laidlaw, also became reminiscent in his last years, and wrote a novel about the Laidlaw family's pioneer experience. Published after his death, *The McGregors: A Novel of an Ontario Pioneer Family* was based, as he says in his preface, "on my own memories and impressions" and on "memories of conversations with parents and grandparents." The family is described as proudly reserved and reticent, with a coldness between father and son: "We lack something, we Scots people. . . . I did not love my father and I fear my John does not love me. We are afraid even to use the word 'love' in the family . . ." (119). Jim McGregor's younger sister, Elspeth, represents a character type also depicted in Munro's own portrait of the self-effacing Fleming sisters (*Moons*). Elspeth is first seen in her parents' house, where everything has been scoured white with lye, homemade soap, and scrub brushes. She is sitting "on the couch now, her feet close together in rough men's boots. Her hands, red and rough from all the scrubbing, were folded in her lap. . . . Her features were pleasant enough but held tightly, as was her whole body, in the tenseness, almost fear, of a wild animal" (48–49). "That's the kind of women we saw around us," Alice told me. "My father did have a family of cousins who were like that. They had a primitive lack of ability to communicate. They just sort of trembled with the horror of [our visit]. My father used to claim in his last years that this was a family characteristic. I have an extraordinary timidity, which I have mostly overcome" (unpublished interview [Ross]).

Robert Laidlaw's own father broke out sufficiently to learn to play the violin and to marry a "tall, temperamental Irish girl with eyes of two colors. That done, he reverted; for the rest of his life he was diligent, orderly, silent" ("Working" 15). Robert's mother, Sarah Jane Code (always called Sadie), was one of four sisters. All four were tall and handsome, reputed to be the best-looking women in the county. Someone had named a horse after tomboyish Sadie in her youth because the horse was such a proud high stepper. Munro's grandparents were prosperous enough to have provided their only child, Robert, with a university education. But at the Continuation School in Blyth he lacked self-assertion: "He felt a danger too, of competition, of ridicule. The family wisdom came to him then. Stay out of it" ("Working" 10–11). He dropped out of school to pursue the solitary life of hunting and trapping in the bush, which he saw through the romantic lens of James Fenimore Cooper's Leatherstocking books. Initially he sold pelts of wild marten, muskrat, and mink, and the red foxes caught in his trapline. In 1925, he bought his first pair of Norwegian silver foxes and started breeding them in pens he built on his father's farm.

The Chamneys: "Daring and Defiance and Escape"

To this farm came a visitor, a good-looking schoolteacher named Anne Clarke Chamney. She was Robert's third cousin, related through his mother on the Irish side. She was brave, prim, energetic, and single-minded, with a forceful personality. Her early experience was the model for Del's mother's story in *Lives*: "In the beginning . . . dark captivity, suffering, then daring and defiance and escape" (67). Anne had come from a much poorer Ottawa Valley farm, in Scotch Corners, not far from Carleton Place. With thin soil barely covering granite outcrops of the Precambrian Shield, farms in this area were never prosperous. The original Scots settlers had moved on to better land, and were replaced, within a generation, by Protestant Irish. The Irish moved in, settled down, established the Anglican Church and the Orangeman's Lodge, and tried to eke out a living. To escape this poverty, Anne Clarke Chamney literally ran away from home to go to high school. She wanted to make something of herself. She may have inherited some of her ambition from her own mother, who had been a teacher. Like Marietta in "The Progress of Love," Anne's mother was a carriage-maker's daughter, coming from "that small-town kind of entrepreneurial class, which has more ambition and is less conservative probably than the man she married, who was a very nice Irish Protestant farmer" (unpublished interview [Ross]). After her marriage, however, this mother became crazed by religion and by an enormous sense of self-sacrifice. She gave her daughter no encouragement, discouragement rather, to go to high school. Anne's father also failed to support her ambition to be a teacher because he felt the daughter of the household should not have to go out and work: she should toil at home until marriage. "Who would I marry in God's name . . . out there at the end of the world with everybody cross-eyed from inbreeding?" Del's mother always asks at this point in the story (*Lives* 65).

Like Del's mother in *Lives*, Anne passed her high-school entrance exams, ran away from home, made herself a dress, and put herself through high school in Carleton Place. As Munro explained to me, "She was incredibly brave. She borrowed money from her cousin, who was already a teacher, to go to normal school in Ottawa. She caught typhoid fever and could not finish her year, borrowed more money, and went back. Set out on a teaching career owing this money, which she then had to pay back. And taught then in Alberta, which was just opening up. She came back and taught in the Ottawa Valley" (unpublished interview [Ross]). She is described in "Friend of My Youth" at this stage of her life, "a young woman with a soft, mischievous face and shiny, opaque silk stockings on her plump legs" (*Friend* 4). Her last job was as a principal in a four-room school. By the time she met Robert Laidlaw, she was almost 30, and had advanced in her career as far as a woman could go. She also wanted to be married.

Robert's mother and this visiting schoolteacher disliked each other from the start, despite being cousins. Sadie probably detected even then unmistakable signs of the desire for self-projection. She thought the visitor was feigning an interest in foxes to entrap her son. But, looking at the foxes, Anne's imagination was actually fired by what she saw as an opportunity for risk taking and wealth. The silver-fox industry was just opening up in the 1920s ("silver" because the foxes were selectively bred for white hairs along the back and tail). Anne and Robert became engaged, and they married in 1927. Money saved from Anne's teaching career helped buy the nine-acre farm in Turnberry Township, the location for the new Laidlaw Fur Farm enterprise. In the twenties, a married woman could not continue teaching, but it must have seemed to Anne that she was exchanging her teaching career for a share in an expanding new industry. She may not have thought then of pens of barking foxes, the need to slaughter horses and grind horsemeat for fox food, the chloroform of the fox-killing box, and the stench and the blood of the pelting operation. Nor could anyone know that, with the Great Depression just two years ahead, they had embarked upon fox farming too late and with too little capital.

Anne Clarke Chamney's heroic struggle — running away from home, getting an education, establishing herself in a career — was supposed to have a payoff: a genteel existence.

FIGURE 4

This studio photograph, taken in Wingham,
shows Alice at about three years of age.

She valued gentility because her own early life had lacked it. According to Alice, "My mother was in some ways very conventional. She was full of self-assertion. But what she wanted, really, was a place in society where you could live in a nice way and have people to tea. She valued material things that would make your life comfortable and would remove your life from all this physical mess that we always had to confront" (unpublished interview [Ross]). Like the mother in "Oh, What Avails" (*Friend of My Youth*), she liked quotations, a favourite being, "whatsoever things *are* lovely, whatsoever things *are* of good report . . . think on these things" (Philippians 4.8). A picture emerges of a woman who prides herself on being different from her Lower Town neighbours. Alice says, "She saw herself as different and she didn't care. We thought it was due to stupidity that she didn't care." Robert Laidlaw, who was "a *wonderful* fitter-inner," had "almost a different vocabulary for outside and inside the house. I've got this myself," said Alice (unpublished interview [Ross]). But her mother made no more attempt to fit in than would a Victorian lady stranded in colonial Africa consider adapting to local customs. Quite the opposite. She deliberately used her correct schoolteacher grammar, which set her speech apart from the rural accent of Huron county. She joined the Book-of-the-Month Club, and acquired a set of good dishes and some pieces of antique furniture. Not able to afford real rugs, she painted the linoleum black with a red-and-white border to make it look more like a rug (then she got carried away and painted "the red and white V-for-victory sign in the middle because it was during the war" ["Interview" (Hancock) 100]). She gave her children a sense of their own specialness. She got Alice to piece a quilt when she was eight so that she could have a head start on her hope chest. She channelled her own considerable energies into sewing elaborate outfits far more posh than those anyone else wore in Wingham, never mind Lower Town. A studio photograph taken midway through the depression, in 1934 or 1935, shows Alice at about three years old, resplendent in ceremonial white shoes, white dress, and bonnet (fig. 4).

"Beautiful Girlhood"

For her first five years, Alice lived the life of a sheltered, cherished only child. Then came changes. A brother, Bill, was born in 1936; a sister, Sheila, in 1937. In 1937, Alice started grade one at Lower Town School. Life in that school was shaming, vulgar, unintelligible, and frightening, but it taught her to build up her defenses. She learned not to confide in people — "you'd be crushed and beaten down if you did." She learned how to survive random violence and squalor:

> People got beaten up. I got beaten up. Before I went to that school, life was cozy and protected. Then at the Lower Town school, no one liked me. And there was the violence and the unpleasantness of things like the outhouse, which I never went into. Since my home was sheltered, things like that would make me feel sick. So those were a tumultuous two years. I can't remember a single class or book from those years. (unpublished interview [Ross])

In "Privilege" (*Who Do You Think You Are?*), which Alice has called "an autobiographical piece, not fiction at all" ("Who" [Gerson] 6), she describes Rose's schooling at a place very much like Lower Town School, with its outhouse smells, lunchpail robbing, and coat slashing: "Her schooling seemed deplorable. . . . But she was not miserable. . . . Learning to survive, no matter with what cravenness and caution, what shocks and forebodings, is not the same as being miserable. It is too interesting" (*Who* 28).

For two years, Alice learned survival skills at Lower Town School, taking grade one, skipping grade two, and taking grade three. But this schooling experience, so useful to the writer, was not the one Alice's mother had in mind. She finagled to get her daughter into Wingham Public School in town, attended by children of a more genteel class. There Alice felt socially dislocated, neither town nor country. She wasn't among the social leaders automatically elected as captains of the war savings-stamp drive or officers of the Junior Red Cross or the Literary Society — these posts went to children of dentists, doctors, and store owners. Being a year younger than others in the class made her feel physically clumsy. She says, "I was always being made to feel like a dimwit. I was klutzy at things." Grade five was the year to start writing with straight pens, which stabbed the paper and dribbled ink. "It seemed to have been far worse for a girl to make a mess than for a boy. So grade five was traumatic" (unpublished interview [Ross]). But, in retrospect, Alice says,

> In this way, I got this look at a big range of society. I was always an outsider and you just couldn't ask for a better beginning for a writer . . . . see[ing] such a big range of people and attitudes and even language by the time I was seven. This is something that you absorb. You use it for your survival when you're a child . . . . I think this is very important, very useful, for a writer. Mind you, it's fairly difficult for a person. ("Interview" [Ross] 23)

Some of Alice's own ambitions coincided with her mother's goals for her. She consistently brought home top marks and prizes for scholastic achievement. She got parts in the operetta performed each spring in the town hall by the senior students at Wingham Public School. In grade seven, Alice was a pirate in *The Magic Beanstalk*. In grade eight, she was a folk dancer in the three-act operetta *The Pied Piper* ("Capacity Crowds at School Concert" [*Wingham Advance-Times* 6 Apr. 1944]), the same role that Del has in *Lives*. There is a similarity between the cycle of operettas listed in *Lives* — "The Pied Piper. *The Gypsy Princess. The Stolen Crown. The Arabian Knight. The Kerry Dancers. The Woodcutter's Daughter*" (108) — and the cycle actually performed by Wingham Public School students — *The Pied Piper*, *The Merry Land O' Magic*, *The White Gypsy* (in which Alice's brother, Billy Laidlaw, played the part of a skeleton in 1947), *Pinocchio*, *The Saucy Hollandaise*, and *The Magic Beanstalk*.

In other ways, Alice strongly resisted her mother's program. She chose friends her mother disapproved of. As a teenager, she rebelled against doing recitations at Sunday school. She repudiated a gift from her mother — a book called *Beautiful Girlhood*:

I still remember the verse in the front of the book by Charles Kingsley: "Be good, sweet maid, and let who will be clever." [laughter] I immediately knew this was a book that I was *not* going to be pleased with. Of course I read it anyway, in a horrible state of anger — not an anger I could communicate to anybody — with a solid recognition that beautiful girlhood was not going to be for me. . . . This book was very heavily into the joys of motherhood — not the joys of sex — motherhood. ("Interview" [Ross] 17)

Aligning herself with the Laidlaw strategy of fitting in, Alice was embarrassed by her mother's theatrical personality. She recalls that her mother used to

come to the school and make her presence felt. I just *died*, even hearing her voice in the corridor, I died. I got the message that she was so at variance with the community. I must have got this message partly through my father's mother — my grandmother — and my aunt. And maybe my father, in some very subliminal way, I don't know. We were *all* embarrassed by my mother, *before* she got sick. When she got sick, that put the cap on it. (unpublished interview [Ross])

Nevertheless, her mother's individuality, however strongly resisted at the time, was a model of confident self-assertion in an environment that otherwise counselled conformity. Alice speculated in 1975, "I never doubted for a minute that my way of seeing [the world] was important, and I really don't know why that is. I think I got a lot of strength from my mother who also never doubted" (unpublished interview [Martineau]).

Wartime

By 1939, Canada entered the war, and lives changed. Wingham boys enlisted and were written up in the *Wingham Advance-Times* — going overseas, being cited for bravery, or going missing. A school for air-force pilots opened at Centralia, south of Wingham in Huron County (*Wingham Advance-Times* 6 Aug. 1942). By 1942, the list of rationed goods included butter, tea and coffee, gasoline, meat (two pounds a person per week), sugar (one half-pound a person), and newsprint. Large advertisements urged readers to get behind the war effort: "Stop this Menace. Come On Canada! Buy the New Victory Bonds"; "Join the Farm Commandos and Help Harvest Food for Victory." When Alice was in grade six, a Doctor Redmond told the Wingham Public School assembly on Empire Day that boys would in future be named Franklin and Winston, "while Adolph and Benito will become household names for our dogs" (*Wingham Advance-Times* 28 May 1942).

The war brought prosperity, but not to the fur-farming industry. By Christmas of 1940, Alice's father was thinking of pelting all his fox and mink, getting out of the fur business for good, and maybe even joining the army as a tradesman. Instead, Alice's mother drew on her managerial talents and practical shrewdness. She suggested not selling the best fox pelts at the Montreal auctions — they should make them into fox scarves and capes to sell themselves. In the summer of 1941, Alice's mother went north to the Pine Tree Hotel in Muskoka, where her refined demeanour helped her to sell furs to rich American tourists ("Working" 37). Later, she looked back fondly on this summer when her bold intervention staved off financial disaster. But Alice's grandmother thought that going on the road for profit shamefully exposed the family to ridicule. And so, at the time, did Alice.

Brief prosperity allowed the Laidlaws to install a bathroom and running water in the farmhouse. It also gave scope to Mrs. Laidlaw's sense of herself as a genteel patron of good causes. In April of 1942, and again in 1943, the Laidlaw Fur Farm donated a scarf of two Canadian mink skins to raise money for the Wingham Red Cross. Through the sale of raffle tickets at 25¢ each, "it is expected that a fine amount of money will be realized" (*Wingham Advance-Times* 1 Apr. 1943). At about this time, the Laidlaw Fur Scholarship of $25 was established to reward the student who scored highest on the Wingham High School entrance exam. Alice responded to this philanthropy:

"That had started when we were in a flush period. It was the sort of thing my mother really wanted to do. And then we couldn't withdraw it after one year. But we couldn't afford to give that! It was *incredible* that we were doing that. That was more cash than I had in hand for an entire year at the school" (unpublished interview [Ross]).

The fact was that the fur business was never financially secure. The Laidlaws were, as Alice put it, "the privileged poor," and when such people become poor, "they are poor in a way that people who are more honest about their situation are not. . . . It also made you feel more ashamed, because the element in this kind of household is the fall from some kind of golden age" (unpublished interview [Ross]). An incident reported in the *Wingham Advance-Times* suggests how insecure the family's situation was. Alice's father and his hired man (the model for Uncle Benny in *Lives*) had been asked by a neighbour to "salvage a cow" that had suddenly dropped dead in his barn doorway. "The fact that they were wearing rubber boots probably saved Robert Laidlaw and Lloyd Cook of town from receiving a severe electric shock or worse" (*Wingham Advance-Times* 3 June 1943). When I showed Alice this newspaper account, she said, "My father might have died. I hadn't known about it. He may not have wanted us to know. If he had died, we would have been destitute."

"Abdication"

With opportunities opening up at the war's end, Alice's mother should have become a great businesswoman. Alice speculates

> She might have gone into some kind of antiques business. I would have had a classic mother-daughter conflict with her, because I would have despised all her values. We would have fought. But there wouldn't have been this enormously peculiar relationship, with all its guilt. And then eventually we would have made friends, one hopes. (unpublished interview [Ross])

Instead, when Alice was about 12, her mother developed Parkinson's disease — an incurable, slowly debilitating illness with bizarre and evasive symptoms that are initially hard to diagnose. In the autobiographical story "The Ottawa Valley," the narrator first notices her mother's left hand and forearm trembling when they are on a visit to her mother's family in the Ottawa Valley near the end of the war. Embedded in this story is a description from a medical encyclopaedia of the symptoms of parkinsonism: *"The onset is very slow. . . . [The patient] shows slowly increasing bodily rigidity, associated with tremors of the head and limbs. There may be various tics, twitches, muscle spasms, and other involuntary movements. . . . The face begins to lose its customary expressiveness . . . . No recoveries are recorded"* (*Something* 236–37). In that story, the daughter's feelings are confused — love mixed with resentment towards her mother, who has "given her consent" to this illness (244) — as are the feelings of the narrator of a later story, "Miles City, Montana," who experiences an angry certainty that her parents had somehow given their "consent to the death of children," to her own death (*Progress* 103).

All along, the watchful Alice had been aware of the dangers lying in wait for her mother, a woman who was so lacking in a sense of precaution and so innocently unaware of how her differences set her apart. Now, like the cholera that had apparently punished great-great-grandfather Laidlaw for venturing too far from home, there arrived this punishing disease. A person, who all her life had wanted to break out and assert herself, became paralyzed and unable to talk. "[I]t did seem," says the narrator of "Home," like "the sort of thing she might have made up, out of perversity, and her true need for attention . . . . This attention was what I was bound not to give, not to be blackmailed into giving. I give it now, being safe" (136). Alice told Eleanor Wachtel that her mother's illness made her very self-protective, unable to afford any pity for her mother because she didn't want to get trapped:

In families like ours it is the oldest daughter's job to stay home and look after people when they're in this situation, until they die. I, instead, got a scholarship and went to

university. There is enormous guilt about doing that, but
at the time you're so busy protecting yourself that you
simply push it under, and then you suffer from it later on.
(50).

There was also the complication of knowing that her mother
would have disliked her writing very much. "Her dislike of sex
was, even for her time, quite violent. So the kind of fiction that
I got into would have appeared to her an insult and a horrifying
waste of talent" (unpublished interview [Ross]).

Alice's complex feelings associated with her mother's illness
lie close to the imaginative centre of her writing. These feelings
are related to major themes in the stories: the loss of control,
associated with death; the desire, as Ildikó de Papp Carrington
puts it in her excellent book, to control the uncontrollable; the
betrayals of language; the humiliation of exposure; the contrast
between the self-protective, disguised, watchful character, and
the exposed, unsuspecting, somehow innocent character; and
the shame of the observer who witnesses exposure. The term
"abdication," which Alice has used to describe her mother's
illness, is also used for love and death (as she watches Char and
Blaikie make love in "Something I've Been Meaning to Tell
You," Et thinks Char has "lost her powers, abdicated," and is
reminded of her brother's drowning: "Sandy drowned, with
green stuff clogging his nostrils, couldn't look more lost than
that [*Something* 11]). In "The Peace of Utrecht," the narrator,
who has returned home after her mother's funeral, remembers
her mother's theatrical struggle against her imprisoning illness,
and recalls her own feelings of shame as an observer, as if she
"were accompanying a particularly tasteless sideshow" (*Dance*
195). What seemed "tasteless" was the mother's helpless griev-
ances, her shameless calling out for attention and love beyond
the power of any adolescent daughter to satisfy. For Alice,
writing was later to become a way of controlling this obsessive
memory, but it doesn't completely work. Hence the moving
ending of "The Ottawa Valley," in which the narrator says,
"[my mother] is the one of course that I am trying to get; it is
to reach her that this whole journey has been undertaken. With
what purpose? To mark her off, to describe, to illumine, to

40

celebrate, to *get rid*, of her; and it did not work, for she looms too close, just as she always did" (*Something* 246). Nevertheless, successive stories from "The Peace of Utrecht" through "The Ottawa Valley," "Winter Wind," "Home," to "Friend of My Youth," recover an image of the mother that gets progressively younger — like Cooper's Leatherstocking, in novels that were written backwards from the aging Pioneer to the youthful Deerslayer. As Alice the writer gets older, the mother in the stories goes from old age and paralysis to youth, until, in "Friend of My Youth," a time is recovered from before her marriage when she is a hopeful young schoolteacher.

Housekeeping

The writing about all this came later. At the time, practical responses to her mother's illness were required of Alice. By 1944, when she entered the Wingham and District High School, Alice, as older daughter, had taken over the mother's role in the house. Male and female roles were then very clearly defined, as they are depicted as being in "Boys and Girls" (*Dance*), with men outside doing heavy and dangerous work and women inside doing housework. So Alice relinquished to her brother the adventurous job of helping with the foxes, and she started making meals, ironing, and bossing around her younger brother and sister. She said, "I thought if I kept house well, then these other disasters, like the failure of the fox farm and my mother's illness, wouldn't completely overwhelm us. It was like a rearguard action." In 1944, Alice's paternal grandmother and her sister, now both widows, moved to Wingham to keep house and help the family. Alice has described them as "these two healthy, hearty, and *charming* old women living in Wingham, when my mother was this incompetent invalid." Very much as portrayed in "Winter Wind" (*Something*), the grandmother and great-aunt represented traditional femininity and conventional values. They were nurturers — great makers of quilts and preserves. They mended Robert Laidlaw's socks and made pies for the family, but were also a source of reproach, making it clear how far short the household had fallen from proper decency and order: "They urged conventionality to a degree that you couldn't deny. . . . they tried desperately to turn me into the right kind of woman. Sewing was the chief thing they urged on me. And they made me embarrassed about the situation at home" (unpublished interview [Ross]).

Alice's energy might just as well have gone into housekeeping when she was a teenager, she says, since it certainly wasn't going into dating boys, "because no one was going to ask me." And why not?

> I suppose because of my innate oddity. Because I was a pretty girl. But the oddity completely overwhelmed the sexual appeal. And the oddity I was trying to suppress. But they were smart; they figured it out! [Which was fortunate] because I was so sexually vulnerable. I was sexually interested, to the point where I would easily have married any of half a dozen people, if they had shown interest in me. I really liked men. I really liked *boys*, and they were so callow. It's just lucky that no one ever made a move. And meanwhile I was trying to get the wash done. And ironing. (unpublished interview [Ross])

"A Way of Surviving as Herself"

Knitting and sewing were strongly promoted by her grandmother as a necessary preparation for being a good farmer's wife. So Alice tried to knit, but not very hard. Her mother wanted her to learn to play tennis as a way of attracting suitable men and moving up in the world — a notion she felt bound to reject, along with most of her mother's ideas. Instead, she read and she thought about stories. Growing up in a community where feelings were hidden and reading was subject to ridicule, Munro was a secret addict, rereading certain favourite books in "a desire for possession" ("Interview" [Ross] 22). Reading, and later writing, became a way of organizing the jumble of experience. She says,

I would even wash the dishes with a book propped up in front of me. . . . I remember being told about somebody named Hessie Scott, who read to such an extent that the fluffballs under her bed were practically as big as footballs. . . . I was constantly warned about the feckless future that was probably in store for me if I didn't give up on reading. This promoted reading a lot with me because, I think, children often want to do what they're being warned against. ("Interview" [Ross] 15)

Five milestones stood out in her childhood reading: Hans Christian Andersen's "The Little Mermaid," Charles Dickens's *A Child's History of England*, L.M. Montgomery's *Emily of New Moon*, the poems of Tennyson, and, of course, Emily Brontë's *Wuthering Heights*. She read Andersen when she was about seven, and remembers not being able to bear the sad ending of "The Little Mermaid."

So I started making up a happy ending and I made up an ending that I liked a lot better. I remember walking around and around in the yard, when I was very small, making up that ending. With a story that I loved, I would go back and read it over and over again. It was a desire for possession. I guess it was like being in love. I could not possess it *enough*, so I made up my own story that was like it. ("Interview" [Ross] 21–22)

The summer she was eight and recovering from whooping cough, she read her first real book, Dickens's *A Child's History*, which she later described in an article entitled "Remember Roger Mortimer" as a shamelessly anecdotal history of intrigues and executions, love stories and villainies. She found out in adulthood that this book, which belonged to her father, had been the first book he had ever read, too — a coincidence not remarked upon at the time, since reading was not something anyone ever discussed ("Remember" 32).

All the more reason why Montgomery's *Emily of New Moon*, about a young girl with a vocation to be a writer, would come as a revelation. Munro says that it was "the watershed book of my life" ("Interview" [Ross] 16). Unlike the sunny Anne books,

Emily was disturbing, with complexity and an underlying menace. As Munro noted in the afterword to the New Canadian Library edition,

> what's central to the story ... is the development of a child — and a girl child, at that — into a writer. ... we have been shown not only how she learned to write, but how she discovered writing as a way of surviving as herself in the world. ... At the very end of the book, Emily writes ... a statement that calmly sums up her naive egotism, cool presumption, and rapturous submission to the demands of her chosen life: *I am going to write a diary, that it may be published when I die.* (359–60)

Montgomery's book shows Emily choosing the black life of the writer and, as Munro puts it, "exultant about the choice" (360). The next big book that she read was a collection of Tennyson's poetry that she found in an old, abandoned house when picnicking with some girlfriends. By this time, she was twelve, and she was writing poetry and reading it almost exclusively. She responded to Tennyson's sad lyrics and long narrative poems such as *The Princess, Enoch Arden, Idylls of the King,* and *In Memoriam,* and tried to imitate lines such as "The moan of doves in immemorial elms." After that, when she was 14, came *Wuthering Heights:* "*Wuthering Heights* really excited me beyond *anything* that was happening in my real life. I think I probably read it thereafter constantly for four or five years. I was really reading it all the time" ("Interview" [Ross] 18).

Reading itself was not enough, and Alice turned to writing as a way of achieving complete possession. In explanation, she has said, "It's hard for me to understand how people, who love reading as much as I did, stop with reading. I would think everybody would then start making up their own stories" ("Interview" [Ross] 22). From the age of 11, Alice made up stories in her head on the long walks to and from school, but she didn't write them down. Some, such as the stories the narrator tells herself in "Boys and Girls" (*Dance* 113), were daydreams. At first, the dreamer plays the hero's role of rescuing others; later, due to her beauty and charm, heroes rescue her. Parallel to these daydreams were imitation stories invented with a real understanding of what fiction is. After "The Little Mermaid" imitation, Alice did imitations in public school of girls' adventure stories and Zane Grey Westerns. The first things she put on paper were poems, which she wrote from ages 12 to 15. Then, all through high school, she worked on "Charlotte Muir," the *Wuthering Heights* imitation. And what impelled her to keep writing? She told Thomas Tausky, "Jack Hodgins said, 'I wanted to be part of the excitement.' That was it. I think there was just an enormous feeling of excitement and wanting to find a place to put it. Fiction was a way of being able to translate a kind of rapture that I think everybody feels. The thing is to find a way of expressing it. And I really felt able to do that then" (unpublished interview [Tausky]). Writing provided a tremendous sense of joy and power. The idea of publishing stories came to her when she was 15, convalescing from having her appendix out: "I had already planned that I was going to write the great novel pretty soon but thought prudently that I wasn't perhaps ready to begin so I would write a short story in the meantime" ("Conversation" 54). Commenting on the story "An Ounce of Cure" (*Dance*), Munro described how the character gets out of a hopelessly messy situation "by looking at the way things happen — by changing from a participant into an observer." This is what she was able to do herself with her writing: "I made the glorious leap from being a victim of my own ineptness and self-conscious miseries to being a godlike arranger of patterns and destinies, even if they were all in my head; I have never leapt back" ("Author's Commentary" 125).

Self-Help

Alice realized that if she wanted to go to university she would have to find the money herself. After the war, furs were no longer fashionable. In debt to his mother, the feed company, and the bank, Robert Laidlaw wound down the fur farm while working from 1947 to 1949 as a night watchman in the foundry. Alice herself worked as a maid for a family in Rosedale, a wealthy section of Toronto, in the summer of 1948, when she was between grades 12 and 13. She felt set apart from the people around her, and the experience sharpened her sense of class differences and provided the perspective for stories such as "Sunday Afternoon" (*Dance*) and "How I Met My Husband" (*Something*). "I didn't know what communism was but I decided I probably was one. I used to preach vaguely left-wing doctrines to the children" (unpublished interview [Ross]). She was already a watcher: "Being a servant in a household . . . you see things about [your employers] that they don't show to people who are their equals, because the ideal servant has no eyes or ears. But I had them!" ("Interview" [Wachtel] 49).

Winning scholarship money was Alice's only hope for getting to university. The high-school exam results, reported three times a year in the local paper, show that for five years Alice Laidlaw shared top marks with Mary Ross, the dentist's daughter. Entering grade 13, Alice won the Dominion-Provincial Bursary, and tied with Mary Ross for a scholarship in French. In the grade 13 graduating class, which had dwindled to 11 students from the 44 who had entered grade 9, Alice ranked first in the dreaded departmental examinations required for university entrance. The *Wingham Advance-Times* listed all of Alice's awards: "Congratulations to Miss Alice Laidlaw" for winning a University of Western Ontario scholarship paying $50 cash and $125 tuition a year for two years, another scholarship of $125 a year for two years, and a Dominion-Provincial Bursary of $400 per year, as well as for ranking first in English of all students applying to Western (31 Aug. 1949).

But the marks weren't announced until August. How could Alice be sure that she would get all the necessary scholarships she needed to afford university? That July, she answered ads in the *Globe and Mail* for teachers for schools in northern Ontario. She was hired for September at a place called Oxdrift, near Dryden and close to the Manitoba border. For $1,000 a year, she would teach 11 students. Then she did win the scholarships, making the teaching job unnecessary, but the scholarship money was barely enough. To survive, she sold her blood for $15 a pint, she picked the suckers from tobacco one summer ("Interview" [Wachtel] 49), and, during the school year, she worked part-time in Western's Lawson Library and in the London Public Library. In an early draft of *Lives of Girls and Women* (in the Alice Munro Papers), Del similarly got a clerical job in the London Public Library, where she "stamped books in and out and rang up people about their overdues and joked with the public and supervised the lazy high-school students." Alice explained, "I was too much of a snob to try for a job in the cafeteria. I thought that will type me: I'll be a scholarship student who has to work in the cafeteria" (unpublished interview [Ross]). With the 35¢ that she could afford each night for dinner, she could buy a tuna-fish sandwich, a cup of coffee, and a butter tart at Cairncross's drugstore. This left her feeling hungry most of the time, although she says ruefully that she didn't seem to lose much weight. "I would sit in the library and be overcome, thinking of a certain kind of chocolate bar" (unpublished interview [Ross]). Working in the library had some benefits, because, as she told J.R. Struthers, she learned nothing at Western about new books: "So the most important work I did here was reading in the library" ("Real Material" 8).

Apprenticeship

At Western, she went into journalism as "a coverup," to avoid having to say she wanted to write fiction (qtd. in Henderson), and switched into honours English in her second year. Her cover in Wingham had been blown, anyway. In grade 13, Mary Ross made a shrewd guess about Alice's future career in her "Prophet's Address," which she delivered to the Wingham High School Literary Society, and which was published in the local paper. Mary imagines returning to Wingham in 1969, encountering former classmates, and seeing, in a bookstore on Josephine Street, "the smiling countenance of Alice Laidlaw, spelt A-L-Y-S, beam[ing] at me from one of the magazine covers. Below her there read 'Candid Confessions honors its most illustrious author. See page 60.' I . . . soon came upon varied scenes of Miss Laidlaw's home life, etc. It seemed since Alice had begun writing for Candid Confessions, its sales had tripled. Her greatest short, short novel which had swept her to fame in

'55 was 'Parkwater's Passionate Pair' " (*Wingham Advance-Times* 4 May 1949). In fact, Alice did experiment with different spellings of her name, and she did try to write commercial stories. When she was waitressing at a second-rate Muskoka lodge in the summer of first year of university, she spent her off hours writing for *True Confessions* magazine. It didn't work, she told John Metcalf: "You can't be cynical about this kind of thing" ("Conversation" 55).

Alice Laidlaw's first published story, "The Dimensions of a Shadow," appeared in the April 1950 issue of the Western student publication *Folio*. Of the 11 contributors to this issue, the first two listed were Alice Laidlaw and Gerald Fremlin, who were married 26 years later: "Alice Laidlaw — Eighteen-year-old freshette. . . . Overly modest about her talents, but hopes to write the Great Canadian Novel some day," and "Gerald Fremlin — Ex-RCAF type, in final year English and Philosophy, whose poetry and prose [have] appeared in Folio and Gazette for several years" (44). Alice was very impressed with Gerry at university, she says, but she was only in first year and he was a glamorous war veteran. She once gave him a story to read, thinking he was the editor of *Folio*. When the story was published, he had already graduated, but wrote her a wonderful letter comparing her to Chekhov. She was overwhelmed — he had noticed her *and* he liked her work.

"The Dimensions of a Shadow," about a spinster teacher, Miss Abelhart, who is infatuated with a boy in her Latin class, demonstrates elements more fully developed in later stories such as "Meneseteung," written almost 40 years later: an artistic outsider figure, a broken sexual taboo, and the easy slide into madness. Ridiculed by the town, Miss Abelhart ends up "alone in a bottomless silence" (10). Alice recalled that, at the time, her landlady remarked of this somewhat Gothic story, "Alice, that's not a bit like you," and remembered thinking, "that's not like the me you know; and why do you assume that's me?" (Beyersbergen). The result of publishing this story, Munro has said, was that "it introduced me to the world right away — to my parents, to the people of Wingham, and to the family of the boy I was to marry — as a not very desirable person" (qtd. in Wayne 11).

A Young Married Woman

Alice met James Munro when she was in her second year of university. She was left wing and he was right wing. She had a rural accent, which she had tried to lose and then felt guilty about losing ("Interview" [Hancock] 95). She was poor, and wore sexy, tarty clothes, like Isabel in "White Dump" (*Progress*). He came from an advantaged Oakville family, and was conventional and rather proper. She wanted to be a writer. His career plan was to climb the executive ladder at Eaton's Department Store, as his father had done. Alice's mother thought Jim an ideal marriage candidate. His family had "second and third and fourth and fifth thoughts" about her:

> *Quite rightly.* I don't think it was the lower caste that they entirely were alarmed by, although that did bother them. But I think there were clear signs that I wasn't going to be a regular-type wife. I had grown up wild. I had this quite mature intelligence, but I had no breeding. So I was probably immediately perceived as a bad risk for Jim. They were quite right; I was. . . . I was very proud of my long hair which was wavy and quite pretty, but it was totally out of style. I was *untidy-looking*. I was sort of big and blooming and untidy, maybe even sexy. They knew right away. Every time he saw me, my father-in-law would say, "Why don't you go to the hairdresser's?" (unpublished interview [Ross])

The narrator of Audrey Thomas's short story "Initram," contemplating a marriage to some extent modelled on Alice's own, is reminded of the 1950s radio soap opera "Our Gal Sunday": "Can a beautiful girl from a poor mining town find happiness as the wife of England's most wealthy and titled lord, Lord Henry Brinthrop?"

But why would a woman determined to write literary masterpieces drop out of an English programme and get married, suitable match or not? She had, in fact, few options. After her two-year scholarship ran out, she couldn't afford a third year at university. "There was no money then to do anything but get married. . . . I could either stay in Wingham or get married"

FIGURE 5

A wedding picture, taken on 29 December 1951, in the
Laidlaw home, shows Alice, Jim Munro, and Alice's parents.

FIGURE 6

*Jim and Alice on Grouse Mountain, in
summer 1953, before Sheila was born.*

(unpublished interview [Tausky]). Nevertheless, at a time when marriage was considered the end of a woman's ambition, Jim always believed in Alice as a writer — not that she would *become* a writer, but that she was one. She says she would not have married a man who didn't: "I personally really don't mind being dominated in any area except my work, and that's when the gates close. Any man who didn't respect my work as an absolute necessity I would leave. No sexual attraction, nothing, would withstand this" ("Great Dames" 38). They were married, in Wingham, on 29 December 1951, when Alice was 20 and Jim was 22 — "a quiet ceremony at the home of the bride's parents" (*Wingham Advance-Times* 2 Jan. 1952). After a wedding dinner at the Brunswick Hotel for the immediate families, Jim and Alice left for Toronto, where they boarded the train to Vancouver. A formal wedding picture (fig. 5), taken in the living room of the Laidlaw farmhouse, shows Alice in a wine-coloured velvet dress with matching accessories and a corsage of Lester Hibbard roses. Mrs. Laidlaw, who was by then very ill, was still able to walk, and could talk in a way that her family could understand and interpret. "She looked quite nice in the picture. She had a fixed look, which is a characteristic of parkinsonians, very masklike. People say now that I'm getting to look like her. I can see it myself. I can see it in the high forehead" (unpublished interview [Ross]).

Going off to Vancouver was "an adventure." "We were very young; we had no idea what to expect" (Wayne 11). Jim worked at Eaton's, while Alice worked as an assistant in the Vancouver Public Library — part-time from February to September 1952, then full-time until June 1953. A snapshot, taken in the summer of 1953, shows Alice and Jim on Grouse Mountain (fig. 6). Their daughter Sheila was born on 5 October 1953, after which Alice worked, in 1954–55, at the library two evenings a week. In the fifties, before the era of reliable birth control, deciding whether you wanted a family wasn't an option. Alice has said, "It's a decision I wouldn't like to have to make. . . . I'm just so terribly glad I had my children when I did. . . . Yet, I have to realize, I probably wouldn't have had them if I had the choice" (Beyersbergen).

In August 1955, a second daughter, Catherine, was born.

Without functioning kidneys, she lived less than two days. The intense grief for this lost daughter surfaced later. At the time, the major feeling was numbness, mixed with relief and guilt. At first, the doctor thought Catherine had Down's syndrome, because the missing kidney function caused the baby's extremities to be swollen from birth. Briefly, it seemed as if Alice had escaped the older-daughter's role of looking after a disabled mother to become a full-time caregiver for a retarded child. Alice thought about getting her name on a waiting list for care facilities, and the wait was six years long. This was not necessary, as it turned out. The baby died and was buried, as was commonly done, in a shoe box slipped without ceremony into an available open grave. Alice and Jim, not conventionally religious, were both scornful of sentimentality, and chose to have no funeral and no tombstone. But until Jenny was born in June 1957, Alice was haunted by recurring dreams: "I was doing something and had the feeling I was forgetting something very, very important. It was a baby. I had left it outside and forgotten about it, and it was out in the rain. By the time I remembered what it was, the baby was dead. This dream stopped when Jenny was born" (unpublished interview [Ross]). A poem in the Alice Munro Papers, written after Jenny was born, is an elegy for the "dark child," who "went without comfort / Without a word to make you human." Eventually, Alice couldn't bear the thought that there was no permanent marker for this child. In 1990, she returned to Vancouver to arrange for a tombstone for Catherine. She says, "A remarkable coincidence occurred: the day I tracked down the records — 7 August 1990 — was exactly 35 years from the day on which I had signed the burial forms in the funeral home. I remember being in the hospital for just two days, and then a few days after that pushing Sheila in her stroller to the funeral home to sign the papers" (unpublished interview [Ross]). Now, in the same graveyard, though not on the exact spot, is a plot marked with a stone for Catherine.

FIGURE 7

Alice in West Vancouver, circa 1958.

"The Struggle Against Herself"

The conflict between writer and nurturer faces every mother who wants to do serious creative work. The time given to the solitary grappling demanded by the writing is time denied to children. And it is not just that children demand to have their needs put first; the mother herself feels guilty about withdrawing to do her work. She must therefore be prepared, as Susan Suleiman puts it, "for the worst kind of struggle, which is the struggle against herself" (363). Munro told Graeme Gibson in 1973 that "in twenty years I've never had a day when I didn't have to think about somebody else's needs. And this means the writing has to be fitted in around it. . . . I think it's a miracle that I've produced anything" ("Alice Munro" 250). Living in a suburb, she told Janet Watts, "My jailers were other women, showing up to have coffee. You didn't have any privacy unless you were extremely eccentric and prepared to be disliked. And I was not. . . . I had a long training in duplicity and confidence, and I led a double life" (qtd. in Watts). In a picture taken around 1958 in a backyard in West Vancouver (fig. 7), she looks like a pretty suburban wife, flirtatiously posed for the camera. Like Jane Austen, who put an embroidery frame over her manuscript when anyone came into the room, Alice protected her writing. She would lie, and claim to be sewing sitting-room curtains rather than say she had to stay home to work on a story. She told Beverly Rasporich, "The dutiful, young mother was a mask for a very strong drive — a kind of monomania about being a writer" (qtd. in Rasporich 3).

When I asked about the personal cost of hanging on to "the two women," Alice said:

> All the heterosexual female writers that I know who decided to marry and have children have the same problem. You don't go into it without this baggage and you don't continue it without this guilt. Every choice you made would deprive you of something. . . . I don't think in terms of a female life without children. So what it means is that you are doing these things all the time that are psychologically terribly, terribly hard on you. You're always failing

somebody. Even when the children are grown. (unpublished interview [Ross])

A female writer may also feel threatened by the possibility that her ambition will make her seem unwomanly and sexually unattractive. Her writing makes men realize, said Alice, that "this still center that they thought was there, this kind of unquestioning cushion, is not there at all . . ." (qtd. in Rasporich 22). A woman within a traditional marriage may see truths that "she would prefer not to see: that she can't see if she wants to maintain her situation." Once you start questioning your life and your situation too far, "your marriage may be in trouble" ("Conversation" 59). So the unquestioning immersion in the role of wife and mother is always in conflict with the writer's detachment, her need to stand back. What gives her the faith to maintain this internal contradiction between the participant and the observer, the ordinary person and the watcher, the fitter-inner and the person who stands outside? Alice told Gibson, "you have to think that your work is more important than almost anything else, and you have to start thinking this when you're very young" ("Alice Munro" 253).

The only person, apart from Jim, to confirm Alice Munro's identity as a writer was Robert Weaver, to whom *The Moons of Jupiter* was later dedicated. An early fan and supporter, Weaver bought her story "The Stranger" for his CBC radio program when she was still at Western. She recalls their first meeting in the mid-fifties. Weaver had

> walked half way up Grouse Mountain to visit me for the first time. I was tied to the house with a very small baby and I had nothing to offer him to drink but tea or coffee. All I had read or heard of editors and publishers led me to believe that they would scorn such timid beverages, so I offered him — *nothing*. Finally in a parched voice he asked me for a drink of water. (qtd. in "Bob Weaver" 13)

With small encouragement from the world, Alice just kept writing whenever she could. She sent stories off to the few available markets, and coped with rejections by focusing her whole attention on what she was writing next — "a form of insurance, really, to keep your sanity" ("Alice Munro Talks" 28). She worked alone, not knowing other writers or feeling part of any community. In 1953, the year Sheila was born, she made her first magazine sale, "A Basket of Strawberries," to *Mayfair*, a publication that shortly afterwards went under. She told Geoff Hancock, "It was one of those heavy stories where there's a whole lot of atmosphere. . . . [I]t showed I was reading the southern writers and absorbing the wrong things" ("Interview" [Hancock] 80). After that, one or two sales a year was enough to keep her going. On the strength of the sales of stories to *Chatelaine* around 1956, the Munros "went out and bought a house"; then the editor changed, and no more stories were accepted ("Conversation" 55). Describing these early stories, Munro said, "when I first started writing, setting meant more to me than people. . . . At first I think I was just overwhelmed by a *place*" (unpublished interview [Gardiner]). (W.R. Martin's book on Munro provides the best account of these early, uncollected stories.)

Munro found a lifeline to contemporary writing in "two little paperback anthologies . . . *New World Writing* and . . . *Discovery*." "I was just reading all the time, being led from one thing to another, mostly American writers at that time. . . . I read all the southern American writers. . . . I was so greedy" ("Interview" [Horwood] 133). The works of Eudora Welty, Flannery O'Connor, and Carson McCullers were important discoveries that confirmed the importance of writing about one's own region, and so was James Agee's *A Death in the Family*. With a good friend in West Vancouver, she would "spend every Tuesday afternoon . . . drinking coffee and smoking until we were dizzy. . . . We read all the books by and about D.H. Lawrence, Katherine Mansfield, the Bloomsbury group, and then we'd get together and we'd talk with incredible excitement" (qtd. in Rasporich 9).

A Delicate Balance

It became increasingly hard to believe in the importance of her work:

> When I was into my twenties I began, as every artist does, to get a much more realistic notion of what [my] powers were. . . . I suddenly realized that writing was going to be about a *thousand* times harder than I had thought and that there were a lot of people out there who were doing better than I was. . . . I suppose everyone goes through this in their twenties. Comparison, the wasted years, all that stuff. . . . [I]t was much more enclosed in the suburbs [of Vancouver] than Wingham was; it was much more *boring*. I have never been able to [do] much with it fictionally because I *hated* it so much. My feelings are all fairly negative, even yet. (unpublished interview [Tausky])

In the late fifties, Munro applied for a Canada Council grant, "and perhaps unwisely I said it was to get a cleaning woman and babysitters. I did not get it, and I heard via the grapevine that . . . part of the reason was that a demand like this just was not taken seriously. I imagine that men who said they had to go to Morocco or Japan would get grants" ("Q and A" 12j).

Until her late twenties, Alice protected herself emotionally, writing stories about people quite different from herself, and avoiding intense personal experience. Then, in 1959, her mother died, and Alice went back to Wingham, to her grandmother's house. Her grandmother brought out her mother's clothes, an incident that became the heart of "The Peace of Utrecht," which Alice wrote that summer. This magnificent story was a breakthrough in terms of the use of personal material. "I didn't really understand what writing was all about until I wrote that story. It turned me around. It gave me some idea of what writing could do, approaching that kind of material" ("Interview" [Connolly, Freake, and Sherman] 8). Munro told Tausky that her early excitement about writing, connected with imitation, lasted until her late twenties, when she became dissatisfied with it and made a breakthrough to a more personally risky kind of writing:

We went north the ... month after our mother
died. It was the beginning of summer, just after
school let out—because no matter how hot the
weather or how heavy and dusty the leaves, I
never could believe that summer began till then
when a general sigh, a loosening of time, seemed to spread
through the streets, and all the shade became deeper
and the sunlight fiercer and blustering, and all sounds,
such as radios playing and dishes clattering through
open windows, seemed leisurely and repetitive
and lakes of asphalt glittered at the end of the street.
We went on the train and it took five hours, not
because it was so far, really, but because the train
stopped at every station and sometimes so to
indulge itself in the middle of fields. My sister Sylvia
got the seat next the window because she was
prepared to quarrel in public and I wasn't. She was
... and I was fifteen and we were wearing, to my
shame, matching dresses of starched blue and
white cotton, with tiny red ribbons at the neck and
a kind of pinafore effect over the shoulders. My mother
had made these dresses last summer—I could,
without shutting my eyes, see the sewing machine
on the dining-room table, that high shabby furnished
room I was not likely to see again.

Until my mother died, though the relationship with her was a very painful, deep one, I wasn't able to look at it or think about it. And the same thing happened when my father died and I wrote "Royal Beatings." These are stories that come out of life. You can't rush them. It's as if until a certain point I was much more an artist than a person. I was essentially fairly tight emotionally. . . . I was very self-protective. . . . I was going through the motions of being a regular person, but the writing was always first. (unpublished interview [Tausky])

Alice Munro, and everybody else, thought of short stories as an apprenticeship for the real thing — the novel. In the Alice Munro Papers, letters dated 1961 from publishers Hugh Kane and Jack McClelland pointed out the hard truths of publishing: books of short stories make a poor start for a beginning writer because they don't sell. So Alice tried to write novels, but they kept turning back into short stories. During the late fifties, she worked on a novel alternately called "Death of a White Fox" and "The White Norwegian" (the manuscript is now in the Alice Munro Papers). The opening page is one of several variant, but similar beginnings in which the narrator and her younger sister travel north to Jubilee to spend the summer with relatives (fig. 8). This was Munro's first sustained piece of writing, and now she says, "It never worked at all. I was writing it all through the summer when Jenny was a year old, so it was 1958. Then my in-laws came to stay for a month. I couldn't get the time to write, but also the psychological effect was devastating. I had to be a housewife when they were there. I couldn't hang on to the idea of myself writing" (unpublished interview [Ross]).

Thirtysomething

By 1961, Jenny had started school and Alice was 30, "An age," the narrator of "Accident" remarks, "at which it is sometimes hard to admit that what you are living is your life" (*Moons* 82). Until she was 30, Alice believed, like Del in *Lives*, that "the only duty of a writer is to produce a masterpiece" (52). After that, she decided she should be grateful to write anything. She had expected to be established by this time, but now it was clear she wasn't close. She became increasingly depressed by rejection letters. Then she acted on Jim's suggestion that when Jenny went to nursery school Alice should get an office where she could write her novel. During her first four months there, all she wrote was a story called "The Office," which she says, is incidentally about a woman's difficulties "in backing off and doing something lonely and egotistical" ("On Writing" 261). She never wrote another word, but she did get her first ulcer. This period of blocked energy, when she felt seized up and unable to write anything at all, was the low point of her life. She says, "I spent hours staring at the walls and the Venetian blinds . . . believing that if I concentrated enough I could pull out of myself a novel that would be a full-blown miracle" ("On Writing" 259).

The solution came after she let go of the fierce attempt to will a novel into being. Jim was the one to make the break. In leaving his job at Eaton's after 12 years and going into business for himself, he went against everything his father had taught him. Figure 9 shows the Munros around the time of the move to Victoria, when Sheila was nine or ten, and Jenny was six or seven. In 1963, the Munros moved to Victoria, and almost immediately found an empty store on Yates Street for their new enterprise, Munro's Books. Without doing any traffic surveys or feasibility studies, they signed a lease and worked hard to build up the business. Those years from 1963 to 1966, says Alice, were "the happiest years in our marriage. We were very poor, but our aims were completely wound up with surviving in this place. It was then like a marriage that maybe pioneers would have had" (unpublished interview [Ross]). Busy every day in the store (fig. 10), and no longer under pressure to write a novel, she sat down one day and wrote "The Red Dress — 1946," followed shortly by "Boys and Girls." A recent bookmark shows the bookstore in its present location on Government Street (fig. 11).

Another turning point was the purchase of the house on 1648 Rockland Avenue. It was a cold, 12-room house aching to be

FIGURE 9

*Sheila, Jim, Jenny, and Alice around
the time of the move to Victoria.*

*Alice working in the Yates Street
bookstore in Victoria, circa 1965.*

made into a showplace, and Alice hated it. She didn't feel up to the splendid style it required. "Once we moved to that house, which we did against my will when I was eight months pregnant, something happened right then. Everything just pulled apart" (unpublished interview [Ross]). She was also physically exhausted for a year after Andrea was born. At the age of 35, she had a new baby, was working part-time in the store, and also had to manage an enormous house without help, except for 13-year-old Sheila, who often looked after the baby. Jim came from a generation of men who didn't do housework, but, says Alice, he was already working incredibly hard six days a week at the store: "There was no way he could turn around and scrub the floors." During this period, she remembers "*nothing* in life mattered to me as much as sleep, not sex, not anything. The marriage never regained anything after that." Jim and Alice would both come home from a day at the store and Alice would start right in feeding the baby and getting supper. "I wouldn't take off my coat sometimes until I'd been in the house half an hour." She says that she grew "so tired and discouraged that when I came out of it I was on my own. Jim hadn't changed, but I had changed" (unpublished interview [Ross]). Differences that could be held in abeyance when they were young and poor, came into focus with their move to the large — and to Alice overshadowing — house.

Dance of the Happy Shades

Alice Munro was scarcely known outside literary circles when Earle Toppings of Ryerson Press wrote in 1967, inviting her to put together a collection of stories for a book. She spent that winter collecting stories written during the previous 14 years, and writing three new ones — "Postcard," "Walker Brothers Cowboy," and "Images" — in response to Ryerson editor Audrey Coffin's request for new stories. *Dance of the Happy Shades* was published in 1968, and was dedicated to Robert E. Laidlaw. When he heard she was having a book published, he said, "Alice, how much is that going to cost you?" ("Interview"

[Horwood] 127). In fact, *Dance* didn't sell well initially, or produce much in royalties — four years later, it had still not sold out its original print run of 2,500 ("Conversation" 62). Ryerson, Canada's oldest established publisher (before its much-publicized sellout to McGraw-Hill), had an excellent record of publishing Canadian writers, but was weak on promoting them and selling their books. *Dance of the Happy Shades* did, however, bring its author immediate prestige, winning the Governor General's Award in 1969. Alice says that before this award her family thought of writing as something she would get over: "So my whole family was very proud. My parents-in-law were proud. My father was *astounded*" ("Interview" [Connolly, Freake, and Sherman] 10). She has said that "people actually would come up to Jim at parties and say, 'I think you're taking this very well,' as if I had been arrested for shoplifting or something. And he wasn't having problems with this at all" (qtd. in Rasporich 15). After this, she had to give up the ruse of curtain making and admit publicly that writing was what she did. When the 1971 census taker asked for her occupation and was poised to write "housewife," she said, for the first time ever, "writer." "The lift it gave me was tremendous" (unpublished interview [Ross]).

This first collection established Alice Munro as a visionary recorder of experience. Many of the 15 stories present a perceptive young narrator's dawning awareness of the powerful and legendary shapes lying behind ordinary life in Huron County. Instead of plots, Munro offers a richly textured arrangement of materials. She told Gibson that she is "very, very excited by what you might call the surface of life," and wants to capture the "exact tone or texture of how things are" ("Alice Munro" 241). In "What Is Real?" Munro says that she thinks of a story not as a straight road, but as a house that you enter, move around inside of, and stay in for a while: "So when I write a story I want to make a certain kind of structure, and I know the feeling I want to get from being inside that structure. . . . I've got to make, I've got to build up, a house, a story, to fit around the indescribable 'feeling' that is like the soul of the story. . . . Then I start accumulating the material and putting it together" (224). Stories often grow from a visual seed, a very vivid scene.

MUNRO'S
BOOKS
1108 GOVERNMENT ST., VICTORIA, B.C. V8W 1Y2 PHONE 382-2464

FIGURE 11

Bookmark from Munro's Books.

Some of the richest stories in *Dance* started from scenes in Alice's own life — "Red Dress — 1946" from her mother's sewing her an elaborate dress; "The Peace of Utrecht" from the experience of returning home after her mother's death, and being confronted with her mother's clothes, the bodiless presence of a ghost; "Images" from the memory of an actual roofed-over cellar house in Lower Town; and "Walker Brother's Cowboy" from the experience of going with her father to visit a woman who teaches her to dance. The major task of writing is to get this initial scene adequately housed in a story that builds round it. Munro calls them "personal stories," because they draw on remembered and invented material — selected, reshaped, and recombined — to convey an emotional reality that is close to Munro's own experience (unpublished interview [Gardiner]). In "Boys and Girls," for example, she wanted to recover the feeling of the self-contained world of the fox farm, with its clear division of male and female roles: "I wanted to get the sense of childhood horrors, imaginary horrors which are a premonition of the real ones" ("Author's Commentary" 126).

Lives of Girls and Women

The next book, *Lives of Girls and Women*, published in 1971, was written with a view to producing the conventional novel that publishers wanted. Never able to work in an office, Munro typed out draft after draft of *Lives* on a table in the laundry room, where heat from the washer and dryer would make up for the inadequate antique furnace ("Interview" [Horwood] 131). She "can't write if there's another adult in the house," she told Gibson in 1973: "it must be that I'm still embarrassed about it somehow" ("Alice Munro" 251). Her material comes from the vivid sensory impressions stored in her own memory, but she needs "a long period of aimless time" to go into her mind, get the details out, and weave them together. She just sits and looks at the wall, "with nobody to notice" and without "an awful lot of pressure. . . . I'm not a relaxed person, so I can't just sit there and let things come" (qtd. in Knelman 22). She writes the first draft fairly slowly, at about 700 words a day. She produces about twice that much on the second draft, and on the final draft, she works "twelve, fourteen hours a day and rip[s] very fast" ("Alice Munro" 252). Writing seems like an enormously chancy thing every time, and not a process she can analyze. She worked at *Lives* almost every day for a year, but the material had been in her head for 10 years. Parts were already written for other stories that hadn't worked, such as the material about Miss Musgrave that was recycled in the portrayal of the Sherriff family in "Epilogue: The Photographer" (unpublished interview [Tausky]).

Achieving more commercial success than *Dance*, *Lives* was the first recipient of the Canadian Booksellers' Award for 1971–72, four printings of its American edition were sold out in a month, and it was an alternate Book-of-the-Month Club selection in both Canada and the United States. Reviews were enthusiastic. When Alice told her father that she had received good reviews in the London *Times* and the *Manchester Guardian*, he said, "Well, you'll never get one in the *Wingham Advance-Times*" (unpublished interview [Ross]).

Written at a difficult time when her 20-year marriage was faltering and she felt powerless, *Lives* is nevertheless a high-spirited book that captures Alice's own adolescent excitement about writing. It is an apprenticeship novel in eight self-containedsections, and presents the experiences of a perceptive girl, Del Jordan, as she comes of age in Jubilee: her encounters with outcasts and eccentrics, her growing awareness of death, her stormy relationship with her mother, her experiences with religion, art, and sexual awakening, and an epilogue on her vocation as a writer. The Alice Munro Papers contain many variants, including some identified as being part of a more conventional novel that was later pulled apart and put into self-contained sections. Munro told Struthers that, despite many attempts, she can't seem to write a traditionally patterned novel because everything seems to go flat: "I don't feel this pulling on the rope to get to the other side that I have to feel. And so I always do the same thing. I go back. I chop it up" ("Real Material" 15).

The copyright page of *Lives* carries the disclaimer, "This

novel is autobiographical in form but not in fact. My family, neighbors and friends did not serve as models." In fact, many elements from Alice's own life turn up in the book in altered form: the small-town setting; the routine humiliations of school; the annual spring concert; the river; the fox-farming father; the Laidlaw penchant for turning down opportunities; Alice's own grandmother and great-aunt, who are models for Del's two aunts; and the hired man, Lloyd Cook, whose stories and mannerisms were used to create Uncle Benny, and who subsequently identified himself as "Uncle Benny." In an early draft, Del's mother has Parkinson's disease, so that her energy is erratic and comes at odd times. In the middle of the night, she might be up "running the sewing machine, clattering pans, ironing," or writing endless letters in her "deteriorating script." But the mother in the published book is a composite figure based partly on Alice's own mother, but more on the mother of a Vancouver friend, who wrote letters to the editor and was "much more political and even more embarrassing to her daughter than mine"(unpublished interview [Ross]). Del is based on aspects of Munro herself — "the emotional reality, the girl's feeling for her mother, for men, for life . . . it's all solidly autobiographical" ("Conversation" 58). A coil notebook in the Alice Munro Papers contains a sketch of Jubilee, showing the familiar Wingham landmarks of the post office and town hall on Main (Josephine) Street, the foundry, the CNR station, the Wawanash (Maitland) River, and the swamp (fig. 12). Munro freely appropriated Wingham because, from the vantage point of Victoria, Wingham seemed like a place that existed only in her own mind, not real at all. "An Open Letter," an essay written by Munro for the first issue of a journal called *Jubilee*, singles out the pleasure of creating a fictional town — "exploring the pattern of it, feeling all those lives, and streets, and hidden rooms and histories, coming to light, seeing all the ceremonies and attitudes and memories in your power. Solitary and meshed, these lives are, buried and celebrated" (5).

The hardest part of *Lives* to write was the epilogue, which Munro was revising, discarding, and rewriting, even when the rest of the book was in galleys. The addition of this section changes the story of a young girl into the story of an artist as a

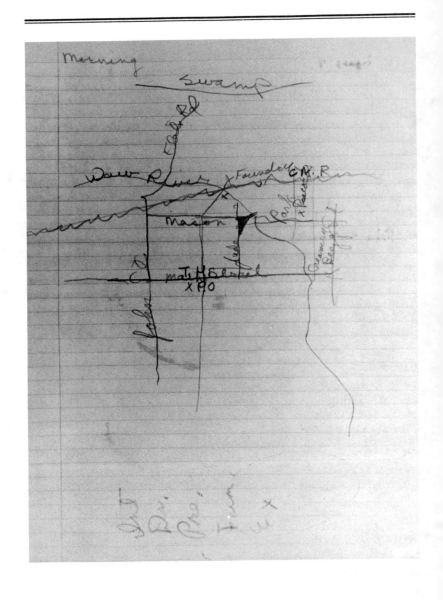

FIGURE 12

*Holograph sketch of Jubilee from a
notebook in the Alice Munro Papers.*

young girl. Munro claims to be dissatisfied with this ending because she feels it introduces an element not adequately prepared for, and yet, she says, "I found eventually that the book didn't mean anything to me without it" ("Real Material" 25). Thomas Tausky's useful article "What Happened to Marion?" quotes excerpts from six letters written to editor Audrey Coffin that record Munro's agonizing struggle with the epilogue: she wrote that the eighth section should be "scrapped" and that the book should end with the seventh section (10 and 22 Dec. 1970); she submitted a new version, saying, "but it's not right yet" (31 Dec. and 9 Jan. 1971); she remarked, "REALLY, we better forget about Marion/Caroline" (19 Jan. 1971); and concluded, "This is getting to be like a prolonged Anxiety Dream, isn't it. I have to *stop*" (20 Jan. 1971) (Tausky 59–61). A typescript of the last page is among the eight or so drafts of the epilogue in the Alice Munro Papers (fig. 13). Showing Munro's careful revisions, this fairly early version does not yet contain the famous reference to the "deep caves paved with kitchen linoleum" (210), or Bobby Sherriff's enigmatic gesture (211), which Munro told Tausky was a turning point: "when that came to me, I knew I could leave it [the epilogue] in" (unpublished interview).

Something I've Been Meaning To Tell You

Describing her bargain to be a writer, Munro has said,

> I think up until the age of forty I would have done anything to be a good writer — really, *anything*. And if someone had said to me, you know, happiness — forget it, forget . . . love, any kind of ordinary life, but you can do a great novel — I'd have said sure. And then that all changed. . . . [W]riters, it seems, have an enormous faith in the importance of art, and then you lose it . . . . ("Interview" [Connolly, Freake, and Sherman] 8)

The balance shifted then between the writer and the person. But Munro kept writing, despite her periodic feeling, ever since a long crack running down it,somewhat diagonally,starting a bit before the middle and ending up at the bottom corner,next to the Chainway Store.

What happened to Bobby Sherriff when he had to go into the ~~Asylum~~ Asylum? What happened Marion
to ~~Marion~~? Not to Caroline. What happened to Marion?

These are questions which persist,in spite of novels.It is ~~strange~~ a shock,when you have
dealt so cunningly,~~satisfactorily~~ so carefully with reality,to come back and find it still there,
diffuse,mysterious,dull,broken,simple,amazing. I did not suddenly realize,looking at
the Herald-Advance wall,and Bobby Sherriff's unrevealing face,that I had lost my novel.
I knew already I had lost it,and I ~~h~~ never did face that fact directly; I just stopped
going to look at it,finally stopped thinking about it altogether,though occasionally I
would be reminded by unlikely things - a board fence,a dog in the street,a phrase in
conversation - and I would feel a quick ache,an almost formal compunction ~~for having let it~~
because I strongly desiring
all die,~~for having~~ lacked the ~~power,strength,~~everything that was needed to bring it to
birth.Nothing immediately took its place.I did not foresee that one day I would be

concerned with that porch where we were sitting,the yellow stucco wall of the house,Bobby
clean beds of geometric flower-beds edged with white washed
Sherriff's mother's ~~beds~~ delphiniums and tiger lilies.Also ~~with~~ the houses on either side,
I just as I would want to re-create with mad painstaking accuracy,a umbrella
the streets.I would want to make lists of the streets,and of the stores and businesses
along the main street,and of people's names,family names,and of the tombstones in the
cemetery,the verses written on them,the names in the cenotaph,the titles of all the movies
that played at the Lyceum theatre from 1940,say,to 1950.Such lists would be a comfort,~~though~~
though they would not ~~inxxinxxxxx~~ contain what I wanted,~~Xixxxxxxxxxxxxxxxxxxxxxxxxxx~~
in the end I would have to see that they could not contain what I wanted,because what I
strokes of light on bark and walls,
wanted was everything - every layer of speech and thought,every grief,~~slant of sunlight,~~
every
smell,~~hut,~~pot-hole,pain,crack,delusion,~~every bug on every leaf,~~held still and held
together,radiant,everlasting. what tricks can manage that?

"Believe me," said Bobby Sherriff wistfully,relieving me of my fork,napkin,and
empty plate,"I wish you luck in your life."
It took them as natural offerings like, people's wishes,
~~It seemed a natural thing for everybody to be wishing me.~~

"Yes,"I said,instead of thank-you.

finishing her second book, that she would give it up. After *Lives* came out, Munro feared she had used up her material. She told Beverley Slopen:

> *Lives* is one of those books I should really have written when I was younger. It is the classic childhood, adolescence, breakthrough-into-maturity book. Every beginning writer has that material — and after that you're not sure what you can do. I went through a bleak period. And then I wrote the stories in the third book, *Something I've Been Meaning to Tell You*, almost desperately. (qtd. in Slopen, "PW" 77)

She wrote them in about a year, but some of the material had been developed earlier. "The Found Boat" was based on material cut from *Lives*. "How I Met My Husband" is what was left of a novel she was writing when she was about 30 ("Name" 70). The title story was another former novel, as she told Alan Twigg: "Then it just sort of boiled down like maple syrup. All I had left was that story" ("What Is" 16).

Something I've Been Meaning to Tell You, published in 1974, is dedicated to Sheila, Jenny, and Andrea, and explores new areas of experience. In addition to stories of a small-town childhood, there are seven stories concerned with urban life, adult experience, the complications of marriage, and the barriers to communication between men and women, old and young. Several stories explore the deceptions and reticences between lovers and ex-lovers, as characters await letters that never arrive or write letters that can never be sent. People look for signs, try to penetrate beneath surfaces, and puzzle over messages as hard to interpret as hieroglyphs. Munro's carefully balanced sentences convey what the characters themselves despair of communicating: the layers of meaning; the implications in the lies, deceptions, and silences; the gap between what the characters mean and what they are able to tell.

Although most of the stories in this collection are not autobiographical, two stories, "Winter Wind" and "The Ottawa Valley," return to familiar material — the grandmother and aunt who represent conventional femininity, the mother with Parkinson's disease, and the daughter who feels humiliation. A new element is Munro's questioning of the legitimacy of writing itself. Munro is apt to want to go deeper, to say, yes, "but this isn't quite it; we may be mistaken." "The Ottawa Valley" deliberately breaks the pattern of the well-made story, because, as Munro told Jeri Kroll, "the writer knows always that the final truth is not to be got at . . ." ("Interview" [Kroll] 53). In "Winter Wind," the narrator, thinking of how she has represented her grandmother's life, says: "how am I to know what I claim to know? . . . Yet I have not invented it. . . . and so I must believe that we get messages another way, that we have connections that cannot be investigated, but have to be relied on" (201). When the writer steps back from the role of participant to watch herself, writing becomes an instrument of exposure and a source of shame. Munro, therefore, has two conflicting feelings — that writing is inadequate and mistaken, but also that it can redeem experience and make life possible: "I have always the conviction, when I am writing something, that the effort and the labour are all mistaken, nothing can work, I am building with invisible bricks. At the same time there is a contradictory conviction that the effort and the labour are most real and urgent, the results unique and compelling and necessary" ("Open Letter" 5).

Breakaway

A woman's success in the outside world provides her with options, which sometimes lead to a marriage breakup. In an earlier generation with fewer options, she and Jim would probably have stayed together, Alice has said. "The differences were not the terrible ones. Nobody was getting drunk, nobody was beating me up, the infidelities came with the dissolution. . . . Jim was unwilling to have a separation. It was all very difficult to pull apart and we'd been together for 20 years" (unpublished interview [Ross]). With three children, including Andrea who was only six, Alice found the logistics of separation hard. For a time, she was living in an apartment and came home to cook dinner for the family. This arrangement was depicted in Audrey Thomas's short story "Initram," which is about a writer-narrator who inopportunely visits another writer, Lydia, who has moved out, but who comes home every day to cook meals. Asked about that story, Alice said:

> actually, in that story Audrey puts real things in and then she invents. The stuff about me having an orgasm in the next room is totally invented. When she came to see me that time, I nearly had a fit because I wasn't living at home. So I had to come home because [Audrey] was broke; she had absolutely nowhere else to stay. . . . I slept on the floor in one of the kid's rooms. But the chicken wings, the kind of dishes, the wine, the coming back home to cook, that was all true.

She now wonders whether at the time she thought enough about the children — "no, I didn't. I thought of myself" — but the result of the separation, she says, was that "we were both able then to become closer to who we really were, whoever that was. And we both married again within three years. I have a strange affection for Jim, which is quite like the feeling I have for my brother. It's irritable, it's nonsexual, but it's very close" (unpublished interview [Ross]).

Despite some guilt over the children, Alice says, "I feel really good about the whole mother part of my life" ("Name" 70). She was determined from the start to give her children a normal upbringing, as different as possible from her own, so that "they wouldn't have any kind of problem from having a weird mother" (qtd. in Rasporich 7). Even so, in their early teens, her daughters would have preferred a more conventional sort of mother. Munro told Barbara Martineau in 1975,

> I think they go through a stage when they don't want a mother who is not shocked by four-letter words; they don't want a mother who reads the underground newspaper they bring home; they want a mother bending over the ironing board saying, "I don't know what this world is coming to,"

because that's something to define themselves against. And they don't want a mother who dresses as I do. I remember I was going out one day wearing a sort of long trailing scarf thing and I said to my oldest daughter, "Does this look too weird?" and she said, "Oh, well, with you, mother, it doesn't really matter now." [Laughter.] I think we crossed the borderline then, and from then on they accepted me beautifully. You know, it's great from the time they're about 15 on. (unpublished interview [Martineau])

As she said to Kem Murch around this same time, "If they still have any embarrassment, they gallantly keep it from me" ("Name" 70).

The final breakaway was the offer of a job, in 1973, as a sessional English instructor teaching a summer-school creative writing course at Notre Dame University in Nelson, British Columbia. At the height of the hippie era, she went off with her long dresses and her three children, determined to remake her life. Unused to handling finances, she was elated to be earning her own money. The woman who met her at the bus depot said, "Do you mind telling me why you came. We didn't think anybody would for this little money" (qtd. in Rasporich 10). They returned to Victoria that summer, and moved into a motel. In September, Alice received an offer of a job at York University in Toronto teaching one day a week, and that solved the problem of what to do next. By this time, Sheila was 20 and independent. So Alice packed her possessions into two trunks and moved, with 16-year-old Jenny and 7-year-old Andrea, to an apartment on Oxford Street in London. From there, she commuted to York throughout the fall until January 1974, when she resigned. For the next academic year, Jenny went back west to her father and Andrea stayed on in London with her mother to attend an alternate school. Alice and Andrea moved to a sublet house on St. George Street owned by a woman who was characterized as amazingly fussy. The renters said they could sublet the house only to a very good housekeeper. "And you're a writer," they said pointedly. Recalling this, Munro laughed, "I thought they might ask me to wash and wax a square of the kitchen floor right on the spot."

Writer in Residence

When Alice accepted the post of writer in residence at Western for the year 1974–75, the Department of English congratulated itself on getting a most suitable candidate to follow Margaret Laurence, who had been writer in residence the year before. Then a junior faculty member myself in the Department of English, and occasionally involved in interviewing Alice on stage for Canadian literature classes, I recall her as diffident about public performances, although always extremely popular with audiences. Accepting the post because the financial security it offered was supposed to allow her to write, she found the public role emotionally draining and almost fraudulent. After talking to groups and answering their questions as honestly as she could, she would "go away and . . . just shake and cry sometimes out of being drained and not being replenished" (unpublished interview [Martineau]). With students who wanted advice, her approach was to encourage writers to find their individual voice by talking about their writing, and by asking what interested them about a particular story. She gave similar advice about taking time for self-discovery when *Chatelaine* asked "several prominent Canadians" to provide advice to Cynthia, a recent university graduate who wanted to know what to do with her life. Barbara Amiel said, "pull yourself together and learn to operate a word processor"; Jack Webster said, "keep an eye out for an older guy with money"; and Alice Munro said, "Push away those voices that are demanding a decision from you now. Take your time, assess your talents, follow your best instincts. . . . [A]llow yourself the time to discover *how* you wish to live" ("What Should Cynthia Do?"). Writer Joan Clark also recalls how Munro encouraged her at a time when she felt stuck. At the summer writing workshop at Banff in 1976, where Munro was an instructor, Clark says,

> I spent a long session with her, and I told her that . . . because I admired her work so much, I was afraid I would just be derivative, and would try to imitate it. And she told me not to worry about that . . . because you have your own way of saying things, your own voice, that will keep grow-

ing as you continue to write — just don't worry about it. So I haven't since.

While she was writer in residence at Western, Professor Brandon Conron of the Department of English nominated her for the degree of doctor of letters, which was awarded on 9 June 1976 in Alumni Hall with the citation, "Here, Mr. Chancellor, is an Alice who, from everyday experience, has created her own Wonderland."

After the 12-room house in Victoria, a rented apartment furnished from a secondhand furniture store promised freedom. In 1974, a *London Free Press* reporter, describing Munro as a "blue-jeaned makeupless woman," quotes her as saying, "I don't think I'd like the responsibility of housekeeping again. . . . I like to do things like make lasagna when I feel like it. I don't like having to do things like that all the time. That's why I think I'll never live with anyone again" (Beyersbergen). Soon after that, she met Gerry Fremlin, who had never married. By this time, he was retired from his job as government geographer, having completed the major project of editing the *National Atlas of Canada*. He heard her being interviewed on CBC radio, where she must have mentioned she was separated. Gerry called up and suggested a drink, Alice took him to Western's faculty club, and they had three martinis each. "We must have both known we were pretty interested in each other, to have had so many drinks," said Alice. In June 1991, sitting in their garden in Clinton, I asked Gerry what had impressed him about Alice. "Probably it was meeting her in the faculty lounge and having three gin and tonics that we got for free." ("Three martinis," said Alice. "We each had three martinis. I had to sign for them.") "Yes, but then a faculty member bought us drinks." ("That was another time.") "So there you are. I saw a whole career opening up" (unpublished interview [Ross]). By the time of this first meeting, Alice was in the final stages of a relationship with a man living in the United States. By New Year's 1975, she says, she probably knew how she felt about Gerry, but wasn't admitting it to herself.

At a small dinner party at my house early in 1975, I recall Alice saying casually, "I met this man again I had known from before." "Yes," said Andrea, in the tone of a nine-year-old who expects to make an impression, "and she wants to marry him." "Oh, Andrea! I do not!" By February 1975, Alice felt that

> doing without men is an impossibility . . . obviously sex is the big thing, and the whole thing of emotions that radiate out from good sex, which seems to me so central in adult life, and so irreplaceable. . . . I'm in a relationship that makes me happy and I feel very secure that way. But there have been times, certainly, when I've felt a terrible fear of becoming unattractive. (unpublished interview [Martineau])

In the summer of 1975, Alice went to live with Gerry in the house where he was born in Clinton, so that they could look after Gerry's sick mother. Living just 20 miles south of Wingham, they would also be able to help Alice's aging father and stepmother. "I never, never, never, never, never, never thought I would end up there [in Huron County]," said Munro (Slopen, "PW" 77). Alice settled into a quiet country life, renovating the house, walking, gardening, and writing. After this move, Andrea lived with her mother in the summers and her father during the school year.

Robert Laidlaw was now married to Mary Etta Laidlaw, who had previously been married to a cousin, Tom Laidlaw, and had kept a store in Blyth. She was a nurturing woman, excellent at gardening, canning, and sewing. She prided herself on not knowing intellectual kinds of things, and she had a challenging style — very much as Irlma is described in "Home," or Flo, in Who Do You Think You Are? Marriage to Etta gave Robert a new sense of fun and freedom. When Robert Laidlaw was about 70, he started writing articles on pioneer experience for a local monthly, The Village Squire, published in Blyth. Just before his death at 75 of heart disease, he was writing a novel posthumously published as The McGregors: A Novel of an Ontario Pioneer Family. He wrote a fairly rough first draft and, while he was in hospital in March 1976, he showed it to Alice for suggestions two weeks before he was to have a risky heart operation. She said, "I've never known a writer more obsessed with his work" (qtd. in Rasporich 6). He rewrote the book during those two weeks, and died about 10 days after the operation. The new draft "was so much better I was astonished. There is no doubt that he could have been a writer, but until I became a writer he would never have thought it possible" ("Interview" [Horwood] 125–26).

Who Do You Think You Are?

When Audrey Coffin retired from McGraw-Hill Ryerson, Munro switched to Macmillan for her fourth book to work with Douglas Gibson, and has since followed him to McClelland and Stewart. *Who Do You Think You Are?*, published in 1978, is, in some ways, a rewrite of *Lives*, presenting material "in a much harsher light" (unpublished interview [Tausky]). Munro says that *Lives* was based on adolescent perceptions of Wingham as remembered from the distanced perspective of Victoria ("Interview" [Connolly, Freake, and Sherman] 8). Coming full circle back to Huron County to live in Clinton, Munro remembered new things, such as a class system based on money, and this darker material ended up in the early sections of *Who Do You Think You Are?* The book is a series of linked, but self-contained stories about a central character, Rose, who grows up with her father and stepmother, Flo, in West Hanratty in a place of "legendary poverty" ("Royal Beatings" 5). She goes to Western as a scholarship student, where she does *not* work in the cafeteria. She changes her rural accent; marries Patrick, a young man from a privileged class; moves to the West Coast; goes into acting; is divorced; assumes roles and strikes poses; and finally returns home, where she discovers who she really is. Dedicated to Gerald Fremlin, *Who* got rave reviews, sold well, was short-listed for England's prestigious Booker Prize, and won the Governor General's Award. In the United States and the United Kingdom, it was released under the title *The Beggar Maid: Stories of Flo and Rose*, which refers to the legend of King Cophetua who, like Lord Henry Brinthrop, married a beggar maid. As Rose says dramatically to Patrick, "We come from two different worlds" (77).

Munro told Struthers that she was interested in "how life is made into a story by the people who live it, and then the whole town sort of makes its own story" ("Real Material" 33). Gerry found a Clinton story in 1975 when he was reading local newspapers as part of a newspaper-preservation project. ("See, even then I was mining him for material," says Alice [unpublished interview (Ross)].) In Clinton, around 1885, a man was suspected of incest. A vigilante group blackened their faces, dragged him out of his house at midnight into the snow, and horsewhipped him. He left town and went to London, where he died in the YMCA of pneumonia. The horsewhippers were tried, but got off with light sentences. This incident is one of the ingredients of "Royal Beatings," presented as the kind of story Flo liked because it gorgeously confirmed her "worst suspicions" (22–23). Alice says it is "the black room at the centre of the house" of "Royal Beatings," and she wanted it there, despite readers who say, "Why write about anything so depressing?" and townspeople who feel that "use of this story is a deliberate exposure, taunt and insult" ("What Is Real?" 225–26).

The book that Macmillan finally published has a complex bibliographic history. One source was a series of 22 sketches called "Places at Home," written around 1975 as text for Peter d'Angelo's "Ontario Photo Album." When Macmillan eventually decided against publishing this book, Alice took portions of the sketches and reused them as elements in the stories of *Who* — the airship over Michigan in "Royal Beatings"; Rose's story about Ruby Carruthers in "Half a Grapefruit"; the stories Flo told about the bishop's sister and about the poison cake in "Half a Grapefruit," and about the seducing funeral director in "Wild Swans"; the cloth hat ("Special headgear or footwear were often the first giveaways" of going off the track [178]), and the old woman in the county home who spends her time spelling in "Spelling." A further textual complication is described in detail in Helen Hoy's illuminating article " 'Rose and Janet': Alice Munro's Metafiction," about an eleventh-hour restructuring of the book. In September 1978, Macmillan sent out galleys of a book for review containing six third-person stories about Rose from West Hanratty and six first-person stories about a writer named Janet from Dalgleish. Reviewer Wayne Grady remarked, in *Books in Canada*, on the "faint Nabokovian twist" at the end of the book when a Dalgleish woman asks Janet, "That Rose you write about. Is that supposed to be you?" But Munro became dissatisfied with metafiction, although earlier, in "Winter Wind," "The Ottawa Valley," and "Home" she had used the device of backing off from her story to comment on writing. Suddenly deciding it was "just too fancy" ("Interview" [Hancock] 88), she phoned Douglas Gibson on a Saturday night. "Are you sitting down?" she said (qtd. in Knelman 16). The changes she proposed involved reworking three Janet stories into Rose stories ("Mischief," "Providence," and "Who Do You Think You Are?"), dropping three others, and adding a new story, "Simon's Luck." She spent a frantic Saturday night and Sunday writing, and arrived at Macmillan's with the changes on Monday, just a month before the 18 November publication deadline. It "cost Munro $1,864" to pay for the typesetting changes that reshaped *Who* into 10 linked stories about Rose, but she says it was worth it (Hoy 59). "I was just very determined" (qtd. in Knelman 16).

Connections

By the mid-seventies, Alice Munro was definitely established as a major writer. In 1974, Virginia Barber of New York wrote and asked to be her agent. Coming from thrifty Huron County, Alice didn't want to pay ten percent of her royalties to an agent unnecessarily. She wrote back saying she had no need of an agent — this despite having signed a contract for American rights to her next book without asking for an advance. Two years later, she changed her mind, which paid off immediately when Barber sold "Royal Beatings" to the *New Yorker*, thereby beginning a long-standing relationship that now includes a contract for first refusal. Munro says that the *New Yorker* editor Charles McGrath always writes, saying "we are so honoured to have your story; it's wonderful; hardly anything needs to be done to it." But then, in a week, along comes a letter detailing changes — Mr. Shawn upstairs questions the need for the paragraph about toilet noises and the rhyme about pickled arseholes in "Royal Beatings," et cetera. Mr. Shawn upstairs, who recently retired as editor in chief, also didn't like stories with writers in them or autobiographical stories, which is why he rejected the autobiographical "Chaddeleys and Flemings." Finally, Alice wrote to McGrath and said, "I don't believe in your Mr. Shawn. You're just making him up. Show me a picture" (unpublished interview [Ross]). The next hurdle for a *New Yorker* story is getting past the checking department, which goes "*crazy* over accuracy" ("Interview" [Connolly, Freake, and Sherman] 9). Correspondence in the Alice Munro Papers contains queries to the author about "The Moons of Jupiter": the father awaiting heart surgery should have been on the sixth, not the eighth, floor of the Toronto General Hospital; the line of poetry he remembers is really "shoreless seas," not "trackless seas"; and no one has thought of the planet Venus as watery for the past 10 years (Alice changed it to "hot and dazzling Venus" [*Moons* 231]).

Munro went on the road herself. From 1977 to 1981, while writing the stories for *The Moons of Jupiter*, she travelled to Australia, China, Reno, and Salt Lake City, but says that travelling doesn't affect the writing. "Bardon Bus," though partly set in Australia, is "much more particularly set in a few strange, grubby, hectic blocks on Queen Street" near Bathurst Street in Toronto, where she often lives in an apartment during the summers (Introduction xv). She went to Australia first in 1979, her travel expenses being covered as part of the award for the Canada-Australia Literary Prize. "Copies of her books barely beat her to Adelaide," writes Jeri Kroll, who interviewed Munro on her Australian tour in March (qtd. in Munro, "Interview" [Kroll] 47). She cut short this visit to come back to Canada to accept the Governor General's Award for *Who Do You Think You Are?* but was back as writer in residence at the University of Queensland from September to October 1980. Alice told Tausky,

I went from being writer-in-residence at UBC, where I was quite sought after and had more to do than I could manage, to Queensland, where nobody had heard of me and nobody wrote anyway. It was a strange, shocking experience. . . . The kids [in Australia] . . . accepted literature as something that great people had done in the past, not something that they could do right now. . . . I really had nothing to do. I just hated it. . . . I felt very dislocated. I managed to get stomach problems just because of the situation. But they were very nice to me. (unpublished interview [Tausky])

On 29 June 1981, Alice left for China along with six other Canadian writers, who were all guests of the Chinese Writers' Association. The book *Chinada*, edited by Gary Geddes, documents this trip with photographs and participants' accounts. The Canadian writers spoke at a formal reception — Pat Lane on the literature of despair, Suzanne Paradis on the Québécois experience, Robert Kroetsch on the tall tale, Adele Wiseman on dolls, and Alice Munro on writing the female experience. Adele Wiseman reports that Alice quoted Jean Rhys: " 'I write about myself because I am the only truth I know,' " and said, "I work in the dark" (114). Alice herself described her approach to travelling in a way that sounds like her approach to writing: "The Chinese wanted to get us from one big place to another, but all I wanted was the in-between bits. I wanted to look into courtyards" ("Through the Jade Curtain" 52). A highlight was a surprise birthday party for Alice — ten courses, seven between-course dishes, three desserts, and some longevity noodles for Alice: "A fiftieth birthday in China? I thought it was gorgeous. . . . Because a fiftieth birthday is something that you're a little scared of. . . . And there I was having this wonderful banquet in Guangzhou. . . . It was the greatest birthday of my life" (55).

Despite this international travel, Alice prefers a quiet life. American short-story writer Grace Paley has said, "I could have written more if I hadn't been out on the street demonstrating." But Alice Munro avoids public causes, controversies, and arguments to protect her energy for her work and for her personal life. She says she knows the limits of her energy: "My solution is to placate people, to play both sides. This was my father's way" (unpublished interview [Ross]). She told Barbara Frum in

1973 that whenever she "differed with a man," she "always tried to be charming or witty about it. I would never really argue because I feared male disapproval dreadfully" ("Great Dames" 38). "I defend myself constantly so my manner is never challenging. . . . I tend to back off from arguments with anybody, not just men" (qtd. in Rasporich 16). In her writing, she also avoids taking sides, because she wants to see a thing all the way around. She says, it is "very hard for me to take any kind of political stand in fiction. . . . Because as soon as I've done it, I would have to turn it inside out. . . . I get very excited about seeing the other side" (unpublished interview [Martineau]). This resistance to lessons in literature began when she was a seven-year-old reading Ryerson Press Sunday-school papers ("Interview" [Connolly, Freake, and Sherman] 9). Likewise, in China, the careful adherence of Chinese writers to the party line she found discouraging. Whether correctness is urged by Methodists, Chinese Marxists, feminists who want only strong female role models, or literary censors, Alice repudiates the idea that literature is there to teach lessons. For her view that literature is "an opener of life" ("What Is" 15), she has been taken to task, most notably in the Huron County "dirty-books" controversy in 1978, when a group calling itself Concerned Citizens fought to keep *Lives of Girls and Women*, Margaret Laurence's *The Diviners*, and several other books out of high schools. Though Munro has rarely involved herself in political activism, she was one of the four members of the Writers' Union who spoke against censorship in a Huron County forum. She still gets "messages or letters from people who say I don't deserve the name of woman" ("Interview" [Horwood] 134).

The Moons of Jupiter

A journalism student in London, Ontario, once asked Alice, "As you get more mature, do you plan on writing more interesting subjects?" and the answer was, "I don't intend to get more mature" (Heward). However, Munro's fifth book, *The Moons of Jupiter*, which came out in 1982, presents characters who are getting older — especially women in their forties, who make uncomfortable discoveries about themselves and, like Lydia in "Dulse," are "up and down" (59). Many are caught up in the voluptuous delight, hysterical eroticism, tearful recriminations, and power struggles involved in love relationships. Creating a sense of life's randomness, the stories focus on the different ways that people get through the unexpected turns of their lives, cope with defeat, survive or not, and go on. *Moons* disproved the claim that readers won't buy short stories. Penguin of Canada bought the Canadian paperback rights for $45,000, a record for Canadian short stories.

Three Janet stories, dropped from the revised version of *Who Do You Think You Are?* ("Chaddeleys and Flemings: 1. Connection," "The Stone in the Field," and "The Moons of Jupiter"), open and close the collection. These three, along with "The Turkey Season," are the only personal stories in the book. But even here, autobiographical material is put together creatively with other material, such as the account of the man buried beneath the stone that Gerry found while looking through old local newspapers. In an introduction written in 1985 for the Penguin paperback edition of *Moons*, Munro addresses again the question of how the fiction relates to the life. If she were trying to write a factual account of her father's death or of the trip to the planetarium with her youngest daughter and her stepbrother, which are elements in the title story, "the result would be quite different, not just in factual detail, in incident, but in feeling. When you start out to write a story many things come from distant parts of your mind and attach themselves to it" (Introduction xiii–xiv).

The other stories are unconnected — an assortment — as are the stories in Munro's next volumes. This form better suits her sense of experience as fragmentary than either linked stories or the novel:

I like looking at people's lives over a number of years, without continuity. Like catching them in snapshots. . . . I don't see that people develop and arrive somewhere. I just see people living in flashes. From time to time. And this is something you do become aware of as you go into middle age. . . . Mostly in my stories I like to look at what people don't understand. ("Interview" [Hancock] 89–90)

Munro, who has always distrusted resolutions and final explanations, tends to undercut interpretations with comments such as, "So she thought." Janet, in "The Stone in the Field," says, "I no longer believe that people's secrets are defined and communicable" (35). Similarly, the narrator of "The Turkey Season" says, "I got to a stage of backing off from the things I couldn't really know" (74).

The Progress of Love

With Munro's sixth book, a pattern was becoming clear: she was producing three or four exactingly written stories every year, and publishing a collection every three or four years. *The Progress of Love*, published in 1986, and dedicated to her sister Sheila, won Alice her third Governor General's Award. Jury chair Helen Weinzweig said: "no matter how she weaves a story, the design is impeccable" (qtd. in Portman). The *New York Times* chose *The Progress of Love*, along with Margaret Atwood's *The Handmaid's Tale* and five other books, for its list of the best fiction of the year. On 19 October 1986, Alice Munro became the first winner of the Marian Engel Award, a prize of $10,000 given to a Canadian woman who has produced "a distinguished and continuing body of work." The award was presented in Toronto, where Alice was participating in the International Festival of Authors.

Only a minority of the 11 stories uses autobiographical and family material. In the title story, Marietta's Ottawa Valley childhood and her religious turn are modelled on Alice's mother's mother. But the central episode originated in a story Gerry told her about his father, who was a policeman in Clinton. Called in to stop a suicide, he found a man on a tractor with one end of a rope tied around his neck and the other end untied. Gerry's father said, "If you're going to kill yourself, you'll have to tie the rope better than that" (unpublished interview [Ross]). Munro first used this story around 1975 in the sketch "Suicide Corners" in "Places from Home" (in the Alice Munro Papers), where the policeman finds a man in a barn with one end of a rope tied around his neck and the other just flung over the beam. In "The Progress of Love," this incident is given to Marietta's mother, but the emphasis is on tricks of memory and the contrasting versions of the event as seen by Marietta and by her sister, Beryl. This incident is thus reshaped to be part of a larger story about, Munro says, "the way values change and the way truth is perceived according to the way outside values have changed" ("Interview" [Connolly, Freake, and Sherman] 8).

With this book, Munro felt she was moving away from personal experience toward stories based on observation and presented on a wide canvas: "I have a stronger feeling for the present — probably because I have used up the past" (qtd. in Slopen, "Look North" 59). "I'm fascinated all the time by the clash of cultures and the changes just in the area that I know. And there's just two areas that I know: I know Huron County, I know the lives of middle-aged women, women of my generation who have been through a few marriages and love affairs, who have children" ("Interview" [Connolly, Freake, and Sherman] 8). Half the stories read like condensed novels: "what I want, you see, is a lot of overlap. I want things to come in as many layers as possible, which means the stories have to come from as many people as possible, with their different baggage of memories. And then I have to hold them still in one frame" (qtd. in MacFarlane 54). As Munro has said, "What I want now in a story is an admission of chaos" (qtd. in Watts). Responding to this epic inclusiveness in her review of *Progress*, Joyce Carol Oates contrasts the minimalist impulse toward "brevity, compactness, artful omission" with Munro's bent toward "expansion, amplification, enrichment" (7).

Friend of My Youth

Munro found her book-promotion tour for *The Progress of Love* physically exhausting, and she always had thought interviews "a lot of flim flam" ("Interview" [Hancock] 76). "I feel blank, that I have nothing to say and I just want to run away and hide" ("Interview" [Connolly, Freake, and Sherman] 10). For *Friend of My Youth*, which was published in 1990, she restricted herself to five media interviews, and refused to go on a tour. She didn't have to. A new Munro book was a literary event — and not just for academic readers. In August 1990, *Glamour* magazine reported the results of its summer reading survey: the most mentioned books were *Friend of My Youth* and anything by Dean Koontz, Danielle Steel, or Larry McMurtry. Although she says she never expected to be a popular writer, Munro has broken down the barrier that often separates literary and popular writing. Short-listed for the Governor General's Award, *Friend of My Youth* won the $10,000 Trillium Award for the best book of the year published in Ontario.

The characters in *Friend* are older, and look back on the pattern of human experience with unillusioned compassion. In "Oh, What Avails," Joan "thinks of her own history of love with no regret but some amazement. It's as if she had once gone in for skydiving" (207). Half the stories are about adultery, prompting *Entertainment Today* to call this seventh book "Sex lives of Canadians" (qtd. in Timson 66). Munro says, "Reporters ask me why I write about adultery so much. Is it because I've had so many adulterous affairs?" (unpublished interview [Ross]). In fact, adultery interests her because it allows her to write about characters who, like Munro herself, lead a double life — the ordinary life and the hidden life of adventure. Another source of doubleness is the tilt into madness, which happens to characters in "Oh, What Avails" and "Meneseteung." Joan thinks that you can look around and see "things in their temporary separateness, all connected underneath. . . . Or you can see rubble. Passing states . . ." (208). Characters tell stories, remembered or invented, as a way of constructing themselves and keeping the rubble at bay. In "Meneseteung," the narrator has partly pieced together, partly imagined, the

FIGURE 14

Alice Munro, in 1990.

biography of a nineteenth-century "poetess," Almeda Roth, from slender clues — a book of her poems with a biographical preface, a photograph, some references in microfilmed newspapers. Commenting on her own urge to uncover the story, the narrator says, "People are curious. . . . They will put things together. . . . just in the hope of seeing this trickle in time, making a connection, rescuing one thing from the rubbish" (73).

After dedicating six books to others, Munro was ready to dedicate this one to the memory of her mother. The germ for the title story was the triangular relationship of two sisters and a farmhand: "Then suddenly my mother's story began to weave around it, without me making a decision" ("Interview" [Wachtel] 50). The narrator starts off by saying that she used to dream about her mother, who would appear looking "so much better than I remembered that I would be astonished. . . . How could I have forgotten this . . . the casual humor she had, not ironic but merry, the lightness and impatience and confidence" (3–4). The mother, whom Alice opposed so fiercely while she was growing up, returns to offer forgiveness and a kind of blessing. She has returned before: in "Peace of Utrecht" as a ghost that can't be exorcised; in "The Ottawa Valley" as an obsessive memory; and in "Home" as a figure in a dream. Munro, older at this point than her mother was when she died, discovered something new in this story: "that, after a while, we don't want the stories changed, even in a better way. . . . you've constructed your whole personality [from a particular story] . . . and you can't quite give it up" ("Interview" [Wachtel] 51). There is an acceptance of the past that brings a kind of release.

Material

Now that she has achieved a degree of fame that would satisfy even that greedy nine-year-old girl she once was, what keeps her going? An interest in everything that is as intense as Dorothy's in "Marrakesh": "beautiful or ugly had ceased to matter, because there was in everything something to be discovered" (*Something* 163). When Eleanor Wachtel asked Munro in 1990, "Are you happy?" she answered, "Yes. . . . It's being interested. . . . [U]nderneath the thing that would help me survive anything, I think, would be this interestedness" ("Interview" [Wachtel] 53). With this curiosity about the world, she has endless material all around her, as I discovered when I went to interview Alice in June 1991.

We had lunch in Goderich. On the way back to Clinton, we stopped in at the United Church in Blyth, where a tea was going on to celebrate the ninetieth birthday of the best man at Alice's parents' wedding. Alice said, "This may be good background for you." A woman came over to the table where we were having tea and party sandwiches and said, "You're Bob Laidlaw's girl — the writer. I thought so, but I wasn't quite sure. I remember your grandmother, Sadie. . . . She had such a straight way of standing."

Another woman sits down, and Alice says, "Is it Nora?"

"Yes, I live in town now. I bought the harness maker's house."

"You used to live on the seventh line. You wouldn't remember, but one time I visited you with my father."

After some more conversation, Nora says, "Last week, I had a party for my eightieth birthday. I had an orchestra. I love dancing."

"Do you still dance?"

"Oh, yes. I still dance. I never get tired of it. I love dancing."

"You tried to teach me to dance. That time my father and I visited you. In your kitchen."

"Did I?"

So there she sat, the model for Nora in "Walker Brother's Cowboy." Eighty years old, with short, iron-grey hair and a face that opened with delight when she saw a friend across the room, she was wearing a skirt patterned with large purple and red flowers. "Do you realize who that was?" said Alice afterwards.

When I wrote that story, I was living in the West. I didn't even change the name, because I really didn't believe that

Huron County existed, except in my own head. I was probably nine at the time of the visit. I made up the romantic connection — when my father married at 25, Nora could only have been 15. But I must have been responding to a sense of vitality and joy. Heavens! I said you might find some useful background. I didn't expect the key character from the first story in *Dance*. If we'd waited longer, perhaps they all would have appeared. (unpublished interview [Ross])

In the garden in Clinton, we tell Gerry about this coincidence. He then says to me, "There's something you should know about this woman; she's dishonest — a kleptomaniac." ("See, I'm fixing him with my steely eye," says Alice.) Then, just before I go, I say, "Is there anything you want to add about Alice?"

"Well, she's very honest."
"What about my beauty and intelligence?"
"Oh, yes, that too."

WORKS CONSULTED

Beyersbergen, Joanna. "No Bitterness or Anxiety for Writers." *London Free Press* 22 June 1974: 70.

"Bob Weaver Has Lots of Friends." *Performing Arts in Canada* 10.3 (1973): 13–15.

Carrington, Ildikó de Papp. *Controlling the Uncontrollable: The Fiction of Alice Munro.* DeKalb, IL: Northern Illinois UP, 1989.

Clark, Joan. Unpublished interview. With Laurie Kruk. 23 Mar. 1990.

Geddes, Gary, et al. *Chinada: Memoirs of the Gang of Seven.* Dunvegan ON: Quadrant, 1982.

Grady, Wayne. "Alice through a Glass Darkly." Rev. of *Who Do You Think You Are?,* by Alice Munro. *Books in Canada* Oct. 1978: 15–16.

Heilbrun, Carolyn G. *Writing a Woman's Life.* 1988. New York: Ballantine, 1989.

Henderson, Heather. "Gently Unsettling Songs of Experience." Rev. of *The Progress of Love,* by Alice Munro. *Maclean's* 22 Sept. 1986: 57.

Heward, Burt. "The Enigmatic Munro: Paradox with a Purpose." *Ottawa Citizen* 22 Nov. 1982.

Hoy, Helen. " 'Rose and Janet': Alice Munro's Metafiction." *Canadian Literature* 121 (1989): 59–83.

Knelman, Martin. "The Past, the Present, and Alice Munro." *Saturday Night* Nov. 1979: 16–18, 20, 22.

Laidlaw, Robert. *The McGregors: A Novel of an Ontario Pioneer Family.* Toronto: Macmillan, 1979.

MacFarlane, David. "Writer in Residence." *Saturday Night* Dec. 1986: 51–55.

Martin, W.R. *Alice Munro: Paradox and Parallel.* Edmonton: U of Alberta P, 1987.

Miller, Judith, ed. *The Art of Alice Munro: Saying the Unsayable.* Waterloo, ON: U of Waterloo P, 1984.

Munro, Alice. Afterword. *Emily of New Moon.* By L.M. Montgomery. New Canadian Library. Toronto: McClelland, 1989.

— . Alice Munro Papers. Department of Rare Books and Special Collections, University of Calgary Libraries, Calgary, Alberta.

— . *The Alice Munro Papers: First Accession* (1950–79). Comp. Jean M. Moore and Jean F. Tener. Calgary: U of Calgary P, 1986.

— . *The Alice Munro Papers: Second Accession* (1973–82). Comp. Jean M. Moore and Jean F. Tener. Calgary: U of Calgary P, 1987.

— . "Alice Munro." *Eleven Canadian Novelists Interviewed by Graeme Gibson.* Toronto: Anansi, 1973. 237–64.

— . "Alice Munro Talks with Mari Stainsby." *British Columbia Library Quarterly* July 1971: 27–31.

— . "Author's Commentary." *Sixteen by Twelve: Short Stories by Canadian Writers.* Ed. John Metcalf. Toronto: Ryerson, 1970. 125–26.

— . "Characters." *Ploughshares* 4.3 (1978): 72–82.

— . "A Conversation with Alice Munro." With John Metcalf. *Journal of Canadian Fiction* 1.4 (1972): 54–62.

— . *Dance of the Happy Shades.* Toronto: Ryerson, 1968.

— [Laidlaw]. "The Dimensions of a Shadow." *Folio* [University of Western Ontario] 4.2 (1950): (4–10).

— . "Everything Here Is Touchable and Mysterious." *Weekend Magazine* 11 May 1974: 33.

— . *Friend of My Youth.* Toronto: McClelland, 1990.

— , et al. "Great Dames." With Barbara Frum. *Maclean's* Apr. 1973: 32, 38.

— . "Home." *74: New Canadian Short Stories.* Ed. David Helwig and Joan Harcourt. Ottawa: Oberon, 1974. 133–53.

— . "Interview: Alice Munro." With Kevin Connolly, Douglas Freake, and Jason Sherman. *What* Sept.–Oct. 1986: 8–10.

— . "An Interview with Alice Munro." With Geoff Hancock. *Canadian Fiction Magazine* 43 (1982): 74–114.

— . "Interview with Alice Munro." With Harold Horwood. Miller 123–34.

— . "Interview with Alice Munro." With Jeri Kroll. *Literature in North Queensland* 8.1 (1980): 47–55.

— . "An Interview with Alice Munro." With Catherine Sheldrick Ross. *Canadian Children's Literature* 53 (1989): 15–24.

— . "An Interview with Alice Munro." With Eleanor Wachtel. *Brick* 40 (1991): 48–53.

— . *Lives of Girls and Women.* 1971. New York: New American Library–Signet, 1974.

——. *The Moons of Jupiter.* 1982. Harmondsworth, Eng.: Penguin, 1983.

——. "Name: Alice Munro; Occupation Writer." With Kem Murch. *Chatelaine* Aug. 1975: 43, 69–72.

——. "An Open Letter." *Jubilee* [London, ON] 1 (1974): 5–7.

——. *The Progress of Love.* Toronto: McClelland, 1986.

——. "Q & A: Alice — An Intimate Appeal." With Suzanne Sandor. *Maclean's* 17 Nov. 1986: 12j–12i.

——. "The Real Material: An Interview with Alice Munro." With J.R. (Tim) Struthers. *Probable Fictions: Alice Munro's Narrative Acts.* Ed. Louis K. MacKendrick. Downsview ON: ECW, 1983. 5–36.

——. "Remember Roger Mortimer: Dickens' *A Child's History of England.*" *Montrealer* Feb. 1962: 34–37.

——. *Something I've Been Meaning to Tell You.* Toronto: McGraw, 1974.

——. "Through the Jade Curtain." With Geoff Hancock. Geddes 51–55.

——. Unpublished interview. With Jill Marjorie Gardiner (Rollins). 1 June 1973. [This interview, transcribed from a recording, appears as an appendix to Gardiner's MA thesis (University of New Brunswick, 1973).]

——. Unpublished interview. With Barbara Martineau. 16 Feb. 1975. [This interview is in the Alice Munro Papers (series 37.20.20).]

——. Unpublished interview. With Catherine Sheldrick Ross. 30 June 1991.

——. Unpublished interview. With Thomas E. Tausky. 20 July 1984.

——. "A Walk on the Wild Side." *Canadian Living* Oct. 1989: 38–42.

——. "What Is: Alice Munro." With Alan Twigg. *For Openers: Conversations with 24 Canadian Writers.* Madeira Park BC: Harbour, 1981. 13–20.

——. "What Is Real?" *Making It New: Contemporary Canadian Stories.* Ed. John Metcalf. Toronto: Methuen, 1982. 223–26.

——, et al. "What Should Cynthia Do with the Rest of Her Life?" *Chatelaine* June 1987: 84.

——. *Who Do You Think You Are?* Toronto: Macmillan, 1978.

——. "Who Do You Think You Are?: Review-Interview with Alice Munro." With Carole Gerson. *Room of One's Own* 4.4 (1979): 2–7.

——. "Working for a Living." *Grand Street* 1.1 (1981): 9–37.

Oates, Joyce Carol. "Characters Dangerously Like Us." Rev. of *The Progress of Love*, by Alice Munro. *New York Times Book Review* 14 Sept. 1986: 7, 9.

Rasporich, Beverly J. *Dance of the Sexes: Art and Gender in the Fiction of Alice Munro.* Edmonton: U of Alberta P, 1990.

Shields, Carol. Unpublished interview. With Laurie Kruk. 9 Apr. 1990.

Slopen, Beverley. "Look North for Writers." *Publishers Weekly* 28 Feb. 1986: 59.

——. "PW Interviews Alice Munro." *Publishers Weekly* 22 Aug. 1986: 76–77.

Suleiman, Susan Rubin. "Writing and Motherhood." *The (M)other Tongue: Essays in Feminist Psychoanalytic Interpretation*. Ed. Shirley Nelson Garner, Claire Kahane, and Madelon Sprengnether. Ithaca, NY: Cornell UP, 1985. 352–77.

Tausky, Thomas E. "What Happened to Marion? Art and Reality in *Lives of Girls and Women*." *Studies in Canadian Literature* 11.1 (1986): 52–76.

Thacker, Robert. "Connection: Alice Munro and Ontario." *American Review of Canadian Studies* 14.2 (1984): 213–26.

Thomas, Audrey. "Initram." *Personal Fictions: Stories by Munro, Wiebe, Thomas, and Blaise*. Ed. Michael Ondaatje. Toronto: Oxford UP, 1977. 161–75.

Timson, Judith. "Merciful Light: Alice Munro's New Stories Are Luminous." *Maclean's* 7 May 1990: 66–67.

Watts, Janet. "A Long Training in Duplicity." *Observer* 1 Feb. 1987.

Wayne, Joyce. "Huron County Blues." *Books in Canada* Oct. 1982: 9–12.

Wiseman, Adele. "How to Get to China: Core Samples from a Continuous Journey." Geddes 98–128.